"Trey, this is Sarah Young, w Perth, Australia. Dotsy wrot. book, Jesus Calling, has been helpful to you. I want you to know that I pray daily, at some length, for all readers. So you have been in my daily prayers. I will also pray for you specifically by name. I am so inspired by your love for Jesus, and your positive, trusting attitude as you go through this ordeal. May Jesus bless you and your family with Peace in His Presence."

Sarah Young, Author (Printed with Permission)

"The Erwin family has touched many hearts because of their faith and compassion, even as they navigate throughout the most difficult time of their lives. They will always have my prayers, love, positive energy, and hugs."

Coach Josh Pastner, University of Memphis Men's Basketball

"Trey was hands down the sweetest and strongest kid I know. He wasn't necessarily the strongest kid physically, but mentally he was and mental strength outweighs physical strength any day. I only knew him over a three month period, but in that three months Trey taught me so much. He taught me to never give up no matter what obstacle you may face. He was always smiling, and he was always happy. Trey has gone away from us, but he's still here with us. He was and always will be my little brother. I love you Trey."

D. J. Stephens, Former University of Memphis Men's Basketball Player

"I was privileged to get to know Trey and the Erwin family during the last few months of his life. Trey fought cancr with the ferocity of the athlete he was. Despite the long odds he was given, Trey never wavered for a moment in his faith in God and His plan for him. He displayed remarkable courage, grace and poise in the midst of such a devastating diagnosis. Trey taught us how to fight, lie and hold to faith and in the process captured the heart of the city of Memphis. Trey's spirit will live forever."

Chris Wallace, General Manager and Vice President of Basketball Operations for the Memphis Grizzlies

"I am deeply sorry for your loss. Please know that all of you will be in Ashley's and my prayers and thoughts during this time. "Blessed are they who morn, for they will be comforted." (Matt. 5:4) I sure enjoyed my conversation with Trey the day I talked to him on the phone. I could tell he had a special spirit about him. I also enjoyed the video special on Trey and all of you. I noticed a poster of me in Trey's room. I am honored that he was a fan of mine, and I feel privileged to have spoken with him. May God's peace be with you. All my best to you all."

Peyton Manning, Denver Broncos, Professional Football Player (Printed with Permission)

A Mighty Dragon

#prayfortrey

The Story of Trey Erwin

By Lisa Erwin

Edited by Rachel Langston

In loving memory of
Trey Erwin

I miss you buddy. I didn't know I could miss you more each day, but I do. I am so thankful for our bond. It was like no other. I miss our talks at night and running Julianne out of the house by curfew. I miss your primping in the mirror right before we walk out the door to make sure your hair is just right. I pray the smile you had here on earth is giving glory to our heavenly Father. As much as you suffered, I pray those who read about you who did not know you will be able to laugh at your goofy sense of humor, marvel at your unwavering faith, and worship through your tweets. I'm so proud of how you marked up your bible and devotion books. It left me with such a treasure to use for this book. Oh, buddy, my heart aches for you. One day I will see you again and we will worship together. That day can't come soon enough. I love you thisssss much.

Dedicated to
My Posse

Cindy Few, Karen Stonebrook, and Hollee Lott, I don't know where I would be today without you. We have cried, prayed, laughed, screamed, traveled and done all the things best friends do together. You have held me up when I thought I could not walk another step and told me it was okay, I didn't have to go anywhere. You've reminded me I don't have to be someone I'm not and I don't need to take on more than I can handle. You have picked up the pieces. It is amazing to see God's handy work in our lives as we walk together doing life. I pray we will be doing life together for many more years. I love each of you very much.

Dedicated to
My Sisters

Donna Thorne and Judy Riley, I could not have made it without the crazy days of your running Collin here and there, letting him spend the night, and the REAL vacations. I know that our loss what your loss too and the pain of losing Trey runs very deep for the entire family. As Jay told me, the way he gets through the day is remembering how Trey handled his days and that makes it somehow better for him. I think that's good advice for our entire family. We have many more REAL vacations ahead of us.

Dedicated to
Julianne Shiles

My sweet girl, we will always consider you our daughter. I love you unconditionally. I know you lost a big part of your heart and I pray as the days go by, that part will heal, but the memories will remain. Yours was a forever love, sweet and pure. Got put you and Trey together for a purpose and that was to support each other. Who else could he be goofy with? I will always be here for you. Make no mistake, that special person in the future will need my approval too!

Dedicated to
Collin

Oh, my little buddy, even though you are bigger than I am now, I know this is hard. I know it is very hard for you to hear that Trey loved you very much. One day you will be able to sort this all out and it will make sense. It may be years and that is okay. I love you just the way you are, as Collin. I am so proud of you! I know God has great plans in store for your life. I love you very much.

Dedicated to
Jay

My dear husband, there are no words to express now much I love you. I don't know how we have made it this far. You are my caregiver and my lifeline. It has been so difficult to grieve alongside of you, yet grieve in a different way. It has been hard to help each other. But you have been so supportive in helping me grieve the way I need to grieve, and I thank you. I never would have thought 20 plus years ago we would be walking this road, but I'm glad I am walking it with you, even when days are bad. I have a feeling the bad days are not over. It is so evident that God has made us stronger and preparing us to be even more dependent on Him. You are my rock, the best dad our children could ever ask for, and a quiet leader. I pray God continues to bless us for our faithfulness.

Contents

PROLOGUE

By Dr. Charles A. Fowler

Seldom are we afforded the opportunity to sense time accelerate and simultaneously feel that it is standing still. It is even more rare to experience those large moments in life with the presence of mind and wisdom to interpret what is taking place around you. Walking alongside the Erwin family through the brief but intense cancer battle that Trey fought was just such an occasion for me.

The only illustration that seems to communicate the essence of that season for me was the biblical account of David and Goliath. When David, who was at the time only a teenager, approached Saul's army he was treated as a young adolescent boy. However, when he recognized that this giant Goliath was blaspheming God's name, a strength of character and conviction rose up within him that could only have come from God. While Saul and his soldiers responded the situation with predictable fear and discouragement, young David defended the glory of God. He walked into battle, not as a young inexperienced teenage soldier but as a seasoned man of God whose faith for the victory was confidently placed upon God Himself. In response to David's faith, God worked in and through him to defeat Goliath and deliver victory to Saul's army.

Prior to the cancer diagnosis, Trey was a typical Christian young man who was trying to enjoy life to the fullest. He was an active part of the Germantown Baptist Church student ministry and was growing in his faith. Then when the cancer diagnosis came many expected him to respond like a typical teenager in fear and dismay but that was just not the case. While others around him struggled with the gravity of Trey's situation, he, like young David, demonstrated a strength of character and conviction that clearly found its source in the Spirit of God. While Trey's journey was very difficult, he walked through it with a maturity that I have seen in few, regardless of their age. It was as if God had prepared him for this season and Trey was determined to walk through it in such a way as to display the glory of God. As I watched the acceleration of his faith which propelled him from being a frail young man facing a ferocious enemy into seasoned man of faith. I could not help but sense that God was doing something very special in and through this situation.

Selflessness has always been a characterizing trait of spiritual maturity for me. In many ways it is at the heart of the Gospel and is demonstrated most fully through Christ's loving sacrifice. As a cancer patient, it would be easy to make life about yourself – your comfort, your needs, your pain, your preferences. Trey seemingly never succumbed to the temptation to make his illness about himself. He always made this about his faith in almighty God who could heal him here or in eternity. It seemed to me, that every time Trey was given an opportunity to speak publicly or privately about his cancer battle he used the opportunity to make much of God.

Trey's selflessness was clearly evident throughout his cancer battle but never more so than during a phone conversation I had with him in his final days. Trey and I had the opportunity to talk privately several times during his illness. Each time he demonstrated great faith, maturity, and a genuine love for his family and friends. I think his understanding of his life situation was remarkable.

With that being said, this final phone conversation was so memorable. He called to ask that I pray with him for his family. He sensed their struggle with his illness and wanted me to pray with him that their faith would be strengthened in order to sustain them when He went home to meet Jesus face to face. The love and concern for his family when his own health was failing was so inspiring and humbling. He wanted his family to be drawn together with a deep love for each other and for their faith in the Lord and love for the Lord to be strong enough to walk through the days ahead. Even as I listened to the spiritual maturity and discernment he was expressing through this conversation, I could hear the weakness and suffering in his voice. His weakened condition was in direct contrast to his faith and selflessness concern for others that were perhaps never stronger. I will never forget that conversation with Trey because he tangibly expressed the heart of the Gospel through his love for his family and friends as well as his confidence in the Lord.

As I close I want return to the illustration of David and Goliath. As I recounted the biblical account above, I mentioned that David defeated Goliath and by so doing delivered a great victory to Saul's army and the Children of Israel. At a glance it might appear that using this as an illustration for understanding Trey's life and cancer battle breaks down because it appears that his giant of cancer won the battle. Praise God that is not the case. Trey was healed on July 5, the date of his homegoing. Selfishly we wish he had been healed physically so he could remain with his family and friends. God had other plans. Trey faced this battle with such selflessness, overt faithfulness, and spiritual maturity that literally it seemed as though he captured the attention of the whole world and inspired them his example. In reality, God accelerated his spiritual growth to walk through this battle in such a way that the God's glory was radiant. Trey used every opportunity as a place to deflect attention from himself and direct it to the Lord. Trey finished his race well. God continues to use his example to deliver victory in the lives of others continue to be inspired. Some have come to saving faith due to his witness. Others have inspired to embrace Christ more intimately and faithfully than ever before because of Trey's example. All of us who knew him saw the hand of God working in him and through him in ways that humbled us. God is clearly redeeming Trey's painful and difficult cancer battle for good in the lives of those who knew him, watched him, and followed his story. This book will simply expand the audience who is welcomed in to Trey's journey of faith. Each one who reads it will be touched by Trey's faith and his desire to not be the center of the story but rather a canvas on which God's glory is displayed for all to see.

INTRODUCTION

We were familiar with the word CANCER in our home. In the back of my mind, I told myself, someday, we would deal with Jay's melanoma more seriously than just making fun of the scars on his head and having to explain the reason he chooses to remain bald. Never, in my wildest dreams, did I think I would use it as a diagnosis for my oldest son, Trey.

Trey was a child who smiled all the time. He lit up a room. In one way or another, he tried our patience by being obnoxious about, what he thought, were brilliant ideas. Often, by the time the conversation was over, I was convinced he was right. If there is one thing I can say about Trey, it's that he loved the Lord, his family, his church, and his Dragons, the Collierville Dragons, that is.

Other than being Trey's beloved school mascot, dragons have a spiritual significance in many religions and cultures and are represented as having wisdom. God prepared Trey to be a dragon of a different kind - fierce and ready for battle.

Many traveled this journey with Trey and our family. Thus, we've included thoughts inserted by family and friends. It is very important to understand that, while God gave Trey courage, Trey relied upon support of his family and friends to get him through some of his toughest days. For Trey, this was a learning experience. While he was strong of mind and spirit, he learned to lean a little too. As he said in his testimony video, "I'm not doing anything but sending out a tweet from a bible verse I read that day and all the glory goes to God in everything. I'm not inspiring anybody. I'm being used by God and I'm just wanting all the glory to go to Him and none, none, none to me."

CHAPTER 1

And There Was In The Land A Mighty Dragon

"Do not be anxious about anything, but in every situation, by prayer and petition, with thanksgiving, present your requests to God. And the peace of God, which transcends all understanding, will guard your hearts and your minds in Christ Jesus."
Philippians 4:6-7

In February 2012, Trey began to complain of a sore throat. Trey suffered from chronic sinusitis, so a sore throat was not abnormal. On February 10, 2012, after several days of constant complaining of increasing pain, Jay took him to the doctor. We, along with the doctor, assumed it was strep throat and left the office with a prescription for antibiotics. They didn't work and Trey continued to complain. On February 14, I took him back to the doctor because his stomach was hurting. The doctor took him off the antibiotic. The pediatrician tested him for mono and the flu and both tests came back negative. The doctor said he probably had a bad virus and it would pass. We all agreed Trey just didn't feel good.

Trey was having spring football practice at Collierville High School, where he played wide receiver. It was the off season and very warm for February. The warm weather was a blessing after the cold of January and they were able to run outside as they were prepared for the spring season. All Trey did was run and lift weights. After practices, he would come home and tell us he had stomach cramps while running and he wasn't able to finish practice. Trey was not lazy and he was very competitive. He was competing with a friend, Corbin Peeper, to see how much weight they could gain in a period of time. Their weights were posted on the board in the weight room and he noticed his weight beginning to drop. As he continued to complain about his stomach, Trey pushed himself to work harder. In spite of drinking multiple protein shakes each day, Trey lost approximately 10 pounds. He was so frustrated with himself. I even teased him and told him I would lose weight if I had to drink those because they tasted horrible. Worse than my teasing was the teasing he was getting from his teammates. What do you think that does to the confidence of a football player? It made Trey more determined...much more determined.

> **Coach Mike O'Neill's Thoughts:** I remember Trey on the track, doubled over, holding his side. He never complained. I could sense something was wrong and instructed him to get out of the drill. We were on the track on the visitor side working on speed drills and improving our technique. Trey insisted that he would be ok and wanted to participate. It wasn't in his nature to give up. He showed that strength and attitude during the entire battle he had with cancer. He made people around him stronger because of his will to fight and the spiritual belief that he would overcome any challenge.

Away from football, Trey could not wait for Disciple Now weekend at our church, Germantown Baptist. During this event, the youth stay in area homes of our church family and come back to the church for bible study, worship, and service projects. On Saturday morning, February 25, Jay and I traded text messages with Trey...
TREY: (with a picture of his urine attached) "You know you are a Tennessee fan if you can pee orange!"

LISA: (thinking it was a joke) "Glad it's not purple!" "Do you want to come home?" "Are you running fever?" "Are you drinking water?"

TREY: "I don't know."

LISA: (starting to get irritated) "Don't know what?" "Are you hot?"

TREY: "Yes. I can't get off the toilet."

LISA: "Can you make it to the church?"

TREY: "Si."

LISA: "Ok, we'll see you there."

TREY: "It's like I have to pee but I can't."

LISA: "You might have a bladder or kidney infection."

TREY: "I've only had 3 hours sleep."

LISA: (laughing to herself) "No wonder you don't feel good."

We made our way to the church. After moving around, Trey felt a bit better, for a while. During one of the services, Trey came out of the Faith Building, hunched over. Jay began pushing on his stomach and the surrounding areas Trey said were hurting. There were a few others standing around and we were all joking about different things it could be until I noticed Trey's color was not good. He was very pale. Jay, a paramedic, glanced at me while continuing to assess Trey. Trusting what I saw in his glance, I said, "It's not his stomach, is it?"

"I don't think so," he answered, quietly.

All teenagers complain, right? Even though we've always been the kind of parents to tell our children to "rub some dirt on it" and move on, my mother's instinct kicked in and we decided to take him, immediately, to Methodist Germantown Hospital Emergency Room. The ER doctor ordered a CT scan and blood work. Trey tested positive for mononucleosis with high levels of bilirubin enzymes, liver enzymes, and pancreatic enzymes. Trey was diagnosed with mononucleosis, told to rest and take ibuprofen for pain. Additionally, the doctor told us to check in with his pediatrician on Monday. Although I took the mononucleosis seriously, I felt relieved we knew why his stomach had been hurting and why he had been so tired. After that, my next thoughts turned to trying not to spread it! Trey was extremely tired, but also irritated he had spent all afternoon at the Emergency Room, missing part of Disciple Now.

"At least I got to watch basketball," he remarked.

He received permission to go back to church, for the evening, but not to spend the night with the group of guys. Trey needed to keep his strength up. Every year at DNOW, a music guest or group comes to lead in worship. Leeland was performing on Saturday night and Trey was excited! After getting back from the hospital, Trey gave all he had in worship and stood on chairs in the back of the Faith Building, singing along with his hands held high in praise. Oh, how unashamed!

Trey came home Saturday night so he could get a good night's rest before returning to church the next day. Early Sunday morning, Jay left for work at the Memphis Fire Department and I decided to keep Trey home. Sometime mid-morning, on Sunday, February 26, the phone rang. When I answered, it was the pediatrician on call at Germantown Methodist. She told me the CT scan had been read by a radiologist at LeBonheur who saw a mass in his pancreas. She told me to pack a bag and head to LeBonheur immediately and he would be admitted for an MRI and possible biopsy.

I was confused! The person on the phone was the same pediatrician that saw him Saturday at Germantown Methodist. What was the connection to LeBonheur? Sometime later, I remembered the CT scans at

~20~

Germantown Methodist are read by pediatric radiologists at LeBonheur. I didn't have time to react. Collin was at church and I put the dogs in their kennels. I didn't even walk upstairs to tell Trey. I called him to the banister and told him about the phone call. His immediate reaction was confusion and tears. All I could say was I didn't know all the details and we needed to get there as soon as possible. When I called Jay, he had the same reaction as I had – confusion! I called my sister to take care of Collin; the news began to spread fast.

When I say the news was spreading fast, so fast that friends, Taylor Wakefield and Michael Penn, beat us to the hospital! We were blessed to receive the most excellent of care in the emergency room. Our nurse, Angela, knew Jay, and an EMT, Melisa, is a friend of ours. How comforting God supplied those people when we received the most devastating news of our lives.

Later that afternoon, a LeBonheur resident arrived to discuss the CT scan results. Thinking we had already been told what it showed, she began explaining the details. I went into a tailspin and started looking, frantically, for Jay. I looked down the hall and I saw his silhouette, standing outside the building in the ambulance bay area by himself.

"You have got to get Jay," I repeated over and over, in between my tears.

I was taken to a private area where the resident told me Trey had a mass in his pancreas, a mass behind his bladder, several spots in his liver and a lesion on his hip. When Jay appeared, she repeated the information and I felt like I still didn't hear her correctly. She was NOT talking about MY son! But she was and, yes, that news was a parent's worst nightmare coming true.

Jay and I agreed the doctor should tell Trey the entire truth. I knew I couldn't speak, or give him the right answers to his questions. After she told Trey, we were able to spend some time alone. This was the first of many times we would cry together. We asked Trey what he wanted to know going forward. Did he want to know every detail or did he just want information on an as needed basis? He told us he wanted to know every detail. We promised him he would know everything and we would never, ever leave him alone. After our family time together, we were told we would be sent to a room for the night and transferred to St. Jude Children's Hospital on Monday, February 27 for an MRI. Doctors at LeBonheur and St. Jude needed to consult with each other to decide the direction of treatment, tests, and/or surgery.

Our heads were reeling from the news. When I left the exam area, friends were gathered in the lobby of the Emergency Room. As I fell into their arms, we told each other it just couldn't be true. It was like we were all in a dream. As we all prayed together, I felt myself go numb. That prayer was the first time "Trey has cancer" came out of my mouth. News continued to spread quickly while Julianne, Trey's girlfriend, was still on her way to the hospital.

Soon, there were kids from Collierville High School, Houston High School and Germantown Baptist Church pouring into his room. The phone began to ring; our cell phones were dinging; and our posse was beginning to form. Again, I could't find Jay. He was not in the room or in the hallway. I checked the bathroom and they said he had not left the floor. Then, I found him at the end of the hall staring out a window.

"It should be me," he said, tears streaming down his face." Why not me?"

I couldn't give him an answer because I was thinking the same thing. Either of us would have gladly volunteered to trade places. All we could do was hold each other for what seemed like eternity. It reality, it was only a moment.

We continued to hear laughter from Trey's room, but I was getting concerned for Trey because I knew he was not feeling well. He was beginning to hurt. As he would curl up in the fetal position, my heart began to hurt, literally. They started him on Morphine, which made him very dizzy and nauseated. He was also becoming very anxious and upset. I asked the nurse for some Ativan and he took that too! Since we had arrived at LeBonheur he had not been able to sleep because of the pain. Now, he was just too upset.

Even in his pain, it was very hard to ask his best friends to leave his side. In fact, one of Trey's best friends, Cody, spent the night and skipped school the next day. It was also very hard for Jay to go home to Collin, who had been at home for hours, not knowing what was going on at the hospital. We notified the rest of our family members and my sister got the terrible assignment of telling my mother.

At some point early in the evening, Dr. David Goshrun (aka Dr. Ross), from St. Jude came to see us to explain exactly what was seen on the CT scan. According to him, there was no mass on the bladder, only fluid. That was answered prayer number one! There was nothing significant about the hip lesion. Answered prayer number two! There was a mass of 1 ½ centimeters by 1 ½ centimeters at the head of his pancreas and there were four to five spots on his liver. Because of the spreading to the liver, they were confident it was malignant. While he was talking, I looked at so many images of Trey's body on the doctor's computer. But it was his words, not the pictures that resonated. Trey had cancer.

What had begun as a 'SURRENDER' themed Disciple Now weekend for Trey had turned into the big "C" (cancer) for a mighty Dragon. As Jay left to take care of Collin, and Trey and I settled in for the night, Philippians 4:6-7 came to my mind.

"Do not be anxious about anything, but in every situation, by prayer and petition, with thanksgiving, present your requests to God. And the peace of God, which transcends all understanding, will guard your hearts and your minds in Christ Jesus."

Cody Jordan's Thoughts: At the beginning of DNOW that year, I knew Trey was feeling sick. The week before, I spent the night with him and he woke up with a fever in the middle of the night. He was still feeling bad that next week, but as usual he put it off like it was no big deal. When it was time to go to the concert the last night of DNOW, I couldn't find Trey to sit with him. I started asking around and overheard someone say he was at the hospital. Naturally, since he was my best friend, I flipped out; I thought he was hurt or something from playing basketball or doing something dumb as we always did. After I heard what was going on, and that it may be cancer, Julianne, Allen Jones and I prayed outside the worship room that everything would be okay and that God's will would be done as we moved forward with Trey's illness.

We stayed for the concert to just fall down and worship before our Lord Jesus so that we could have some sense of peace with it all. During the concert, I knelt down and opened my bible to a random page and started reading, exactly what God wanted me to do in that moment. After that, I went to the hospital and saw Trey. While we were sitting there talking, I felt God lead me to tell Trey the verse that I just happened to flip open my bible to. James 1:2-3 says, "Consider it all joy, my brethren, when you encounter various trials, knowing that the testing of your faith produces endurance."

What I didn't realize is that God would use this verse through Trey's battle with cancer to lift him up and become a statement to our community that all of Trey's hope and peace was with God, no matter what happened. One night, in particular, sticks out in my mind while Trey was still at LeBonheur Children's Research Hospital in Memphis. I was scared and upset at what was going on with my best friend so, I stayed a night in the hospital and skipped school and work the next day to spend some time with Trey. I show up and Trey and I are talking on and on about whatever. I remember laughing and just having a good time and seeing that guy smile while he was hurting so much still makes me happy to this day.

We fell asleep together on his hospital bed and I woke up in the middle of the night and moved to the chair/bed thing they had there. When we woke up the next morning we heard St. Jude would be sending a consultant to talk to us about what going on with him. They guy came in and he was the most peppy person I have seen in my life. I don't think he realized how old Trey was because he was using terms like tummy and pee-pee to describe things and all Trey could do was smile and laugh a little bit. After that happened, the consultant confirmed that there was a good chance that Trey had cancer and that St. Jude wanted to take him in as a patient. It was one of very few times I remember Trey getting upset and hanging his head.

Trey was one of those people that didn't SAY he was upset. I had to watch his face and body language to figure if he was ACTUALLY okay or not with what was happening at the time. I had to leave a couple hours later. Before that, Trey played a joke on me and Julianne and the others that were there.

CHAPTER 2

ISN'T ST. JUDE FOR LITTLE PEOPLE?

"For where two or three have gathered together in My name, I am there in their midst."
Matthew 18:20

February 27, 2012

On February 27, Trey tweeted *"Too blessed to be stressed. Headed to St. Jude today."* Actually, we didn't get to St. Jude until Tuesday, February 28. We were ready to get the ball rolling and begin giving God the glory for Trey's healing. They buckled Trey up like he was going to parachute out of his gurney and all we could do was laugh and take pictures! I got that big smile and his signature two thumbs up that said, "I can do this Mom!"

We arrived at St. Jude and the colors on the walls were so vivid. Trey and I laughed because we felt like we had just walked out of the house in the "Wizard of Oz" movie. There were toy boats you could crawl in, blocks, and coloring areas with all kinds of toys. We saw little children being rolled down the halls in little red wagons hooked up to tubes that ran to poles. Then, I saw a teenager with headphones on but he didn't have any hair! My heart sank to my toes. My son was rolling in with a full head of the most gorgeous brown "Beiber" hair. After all, the Beibs was his nickname! He had been made fun of all his life for his head full of hair. I remember days he would come home crying because of the names his, so called, friends called him. I told Trey they were just jealous! Now, all I could do was look at the floor until we got to our room. I felt so sorry for this young boy with no hair.

Trey, with his remarkable wit, said, "I'm going to get kicked out of St. Jude because I have hair!"

> **Coach Mike O'Neill's Thoughts:** My first memory of Trey was when he attended our conditioning program after his freshman season. The seniors, including my own son, kept calling one of the incoming varsity players- Bieber. This player had Justin Bieber hair and smiled all of the time. The only reason I knew because my daughter was a hug fan of Justin Bieber and had posters all over her wall. They were right on! I could not help but laugh.

While we were there, it's not like I didn't see small children without hair, but the teenager struck a chord in me that touched my heart.

We were told Trey was scheduled for an MRI and we would get the results that afternoon. This would be the first diagnostic test and we were very anxious to have this done. But, the MRI didn't happen on Tuesday. We didn't understand why. We were told it was scheduled! We were told this was so important! Don't they know he has cancer?

Trey's spiritual strength was already becoming evident. He had the courage of a lion and a faith in the Lord that amazed everyone he met. He was so blessed to have such loving friends. We never kept the visitors away and his countenance changed when people walked in the room. I don't know if it was Trey or his friends who did the most encouraging. Nurses at St. Jude commented they had not seen such an outpouring of love for one patient before. They were so tolerant with our crowds and our laughter.

We saw many doctors within hours of entering St. Jude - surgeons, oncologists, residents, and fellows. What in the world is a fellow? Each one would enter the room saying, "Hello, I am Jerry's _____."

Before they could finish the sentence, Trey would answer, "My name is Trey."

Someone told me to get a notepad and write things down as doctors and nurses came in during the day and night. You've got to be kidding me! There's not enough time to write it all down. I started making sure someone was in the room with me to help listen and I learned, if I didn't get anything else, to write down the names and telephone numbers of doctors. That was enough!

Among God's first blessings was Dr. Sara Federico, Trey's pediatric oncologist. We all clicked immediately. There was just something about her. She had a kind face, yet, when she walked in the room, it lit up like fireworks were going off. Dr. Sara's personality was always positive and upbeat. She was infectious!

She told us we were scheduled for an MRI at 10 a.m. on Wednesday morning. He was also scheduled for a PET scan and a chest x-ray on Friday, March 2. They also told us he would have a biopsy that week, but only after they knew which area to biopsy - the pancreas or liver.

"Why not just biopsy the pancreas?", I asked, over and over.

I didn't realize how volatile the pancreas could be. A tiny organ, no bigger than six inches in length, could determine my son's future. Quickly, we learned to expect several changes before anything "scheduled" really happened. Sometimes it was comical. Sometimes, it was frustrating.

During this evaluation process, we told the doctors today about a blow to he recently received to the abdomen at a basketball game. The doctors told us a sharp blow in just the right place could cause pancreatitis and/or bruising. That was encouraging news! I remember the night he passed out at the high school game after he received the hit to his abdomen. That was so unlike him. He was just standing in the student section and was hit in the abdomen then passed out.

Early on, doctors told us Trey's case was very rare, but we didn't fully understand why. As far as we knew, they had only done a few tests! They told us they have not seen a pancreatic case such as this in a child in many years. We immediately began to ask our prayer warriors to pray for wisdom! We knew God could do anything including heal him. We were also praying the PET scan would not show any additional hot spots of cancer in his body. We knew what a PET scan would show since we had already been told of the spots on his liver.

We had to explain the family cancer history to each doctor beginning with the fact that Jay was not in remission from melanoma but it had not metastasized. Jay's brother, Barry, died at age 22 of Hodgkin's disease and was a St. Jude patient. He also had melanoma. Jay's father, Jerry, died in 2008 of cancer and also had melanoma. Things were not adding up.

We have tried to make his room as comfortable as possible. One of his friends brought a poster board so visitors can write notes on the poster. I thought that was a great idea. There are so many times Trey is in pain and sleeping when people arrive, but we are not turning his friends away.

We began asking people to Pray for Trey! On Monday night, friends, neighbors and Christian brothers and sisters responded to our request by holding a prayer vigil on our front yard. Humbled, my thoughts were pieces of scripture…

"Our God reigns!"

"Ask and you shall receive!"

"Where two or more are gathered together, He is there also!"

The prayers for our family and messages of encouragement were beyond imagination. The twitter hashtag #prayfortrey started gaining momentum. Trey's response on Twitter was *"So incredibly blessed with so many friends. Can't describe how thankful I am. #loveyall."* Trey was thankful, but anxious at the same time to see his Collierville football teammates when they came to visit. It was unforgettable. It was a visit that helped him feel a little normal again, the laughter. I could sense the boys were uncomfortable because they didn't know exactly what to say. Trey kept his sense of humor during the chaos. Someone from the football team said if Trey loses his hair, they will shave their head. Trey immediately tweeted, *"Hey guys...I'm not getting a haircut for a while...so uh...you don't have to shave your head...hahaha."* Trey's hair is sacred! I've always told him he was my Samson and I just might sneak in his room one night, cut his hair and take all his strength.

Trey kept asking for Collin. We knew at some point, we would need to explain everything to him. Trey was so concerned Collin would not understand. We told Trey over and over again Collin was much smarter than he gave him credit for. Keith (our Student Pastor) and Bretta, our dear friends, checked him out of school and brought him to St. Jude just so he could be with Trey.

Jay and I took Collin down the hall to the sitting area and had a very simple conversation with him. There was no need to get into details at this point because there would be questions that even we could not answer. Some questions from Collin were easy, but Collin is very quiet and we know we will have time to talk. The most important thing was Trey and Collin together watching movies. Something they did all the time.

While Trey and Collin were watching movies, the college ministry of Germantown Baptist Church, unknown to us, were praying in each room of our home. If I had known, I would have been mortified. Afterwards, I thought what a loving, selfless thing to do. As I looked at pictures of these students laying hands on Trey's bed and praying, all I remembered were Matthew's words *"For where two or three have gathered together in My name, I am there in their midst."* Matthew 18:20.

Trey kept saying, "I'm gonna be fine. If I get sick and have to take medicine, I'll sleep and be fine. If I'm in pain, I'll take medicine and be fine. If they don't find anything, I'll be fine. If I don't make it, I'll even be better. Mom, I'll be fine." I got so irritated and felt like he was being a flippant teenager or in some degree of denial. Eventually, I told him I understoodwhat he meant when he said "I'll be fine Mom". He gets it.

Numbers and medical terminology began to become very important to us. It flew out of the doctors mouths so fast I didn't have time to write it down. So every morning after they took his blood at 4 a.m., I asked for a copy of his labs around 8 or 9 a.m. We met one the person who would be one of our biggest advocates, Karen Williams, a nurse practitioner in the Quality of Life department. If I had any questions, Karen was there to answer any of our medical questions at any time, buy phone or text. Unfortunately, her title means exactly what it says. Helping patients have the best quality of life with the time they have left. She formed a bond with Trey and our family by helping us understand what we were going through on a daily basis. There were no medical hidden agendas.

The terms we were hearing frequently were lipase and amylase. Lipase is an enzyme released by the pancreas into the small intestine to help absorb fat by breaking down fat into fatty acids. The amylase enzyme is secreted through the pancreatic duct into the duodenum where it helps break down dietary carbohydrates. Lipase counts should be around 100. Yesterday they were at 4,000. Today he was at 2,000. We were told, because his pancreas was very aggravated, the counts would fluctuate. After the 12 vials of blood they took, I wonder if there is anything left to fluctuate!

We learned when these numbers were running high, Trey was in pain and needed to have his pain medication increased. Understanding these circumstances did not prevent anxiety. I could see Trey was beginning to experience a little bit of anxiety and requested Ativan to help him sleep. Trey was also just learning the names of medications and why they were used. Nausea is such a demon of this disease, so the nurses were on top of that too.

The most frustrating thing for Trey was he could not eat. Because of upcoming tests, he was on a liquid diet and was not a happy camper! When he could eat, his diet was restricted to low fat. Believe me, we were dealing with one hungry, upset teenage boy! The only thing he took comfort in was Jello snack packs. Morning, noon, and night, he ate snack packs. Call Bill Cosby!!!! We need stock in Jello!

CHAPTER 3

#prayfortrey

"Trust in the LORD with all your heart And do not lean on your own understanding. In all your ways acknowledge Him, And He will make your paths straight." Proverbs 3:5-6

February 29, 2012

Trey went for his MRI this morning. We were told it could take an hour or more for them to do the MRI. He had no problem getting on the table, but staying comfortable on the table for that length of time was an issue. The average amount of slides taken for an MRI is 100. For Trey, they took over 1,000. No wonder he had to lie there so long!

The hashtag #prayfortrey is all over Twitter and adults have begun to ask about Twitter, what it is and how to use it. We know our prayer warriors are watching each post. Trey tweeted. *"Know(ing) that God is using you is the best feeling anyone could ever have."*

This afternoon, we were contacted by a reporter from Channel 5 news. They told us they had interviewed Mike O'Neill at Collierville High School, Trey's football coach. We know God is beginning a work in the hearts of His people! We are so excited to tell about the prayers going up for Trey.

Trey is scheduled for a liver biopsy for tomorrow and a procedure to receive a central line called a Hickman. Hopefully, after this, he can eat.

Trey tweeted, *"Man, I didn't do anything, this is the Lord's work."*

Later in the day, the MRI results came back showing no cancer in the pancreas. We were all relieved and confident. God is still in the business of miracles! When the doctor from Methodist told us, I screamed and cried at the same time.

Trey keeps saying, "I told you so." That's one smart remark I'll accept.

He has been diagnosed with pancreas divisum, a birth defect which causes the pancreas not to drain properly into the liver. It needs to be fixed by surgery or by a scope, but not at St. Jude. The doctor that will perform the procedure came by to let us know the procedure will be done at Methodist Central. The doctor will be reading his scans tonight or tomorrow and let us know if we need anything before we leave St. Jude.

I liked hearing the words **leave St. Jude**. At this point, the verse in my head was *"The prayers of the righteous availeth much."* James 5:16. Thank you, Lord.

Additionally, there were four or five spots on the edge of the liver, which they believe to be hemangiomas. One other spot on the liver was cause for concern and we found ourselves waiting for results of another scan. We handled each period of waiting a little better. During the wait, Trey tweeted *"Still have a journey to go #prayersstillneeded"*

If it weren't for the many visitors, I think we'd go crazy on this emotional roller coaster! One doctor says no cancer. Then, another comes in to say that it's not 100% certain. I told his oncologist we'd go with NO CANCER, especially since they said they have never seen this in a child so young. According to statistics, Trey is one in 5,000,000. Someone mentioned they had not seen a case of pancreatic cancer in a child since the 1970's. This was too rare. The oncologist agreed and told us to jump on that!

The reporter from Channel 5 news called back. I told her we had been told he had no cancer and we believed it was a result of the prayers to God from so many people. She said they were going to pull the story. What? God isn't newsworthy? Our community coming together in prayer isn't newsworthy?

The plan was to go home tomorrow and follow up with the doctor from Methodist. Trey is ready to eat and sleep in his own bed.

I am having faith God will continue His work through Trey and heal him completely with no doubts. He is showing himself in a mighty way.

I have called on every prayer warrior to help us pray. We are not out of the woods. The St. Jude doctors keep apologizing to us for the roller coaster of emotions we were on. That is an accurate description! The texts, emails, and posts to Caringbridge are coming too fast for me to respond and answering the easiest of questions is a difficult task. When Trey asked why I set up a Caringbridge page, I told him the time had come when I needed to answer many questions at once, instead of one at a time.

It was not a good night and I struggled to understand how things can change so fast. His lipase counts tripled overnight from 1,000 to 3,000, indicating problems with the pancreas. The doctors thought it could be from what from Trey ate, but he only had a bite of cake and jello.

Trey does not get angry or sad very easily, but not being able to eat is taking its toll on him. He's counting the days of not being able to eat because Jello snack packs are not eating to him. At this point, he would even eat cafeteria food. Unfortunately, in case of a liver biopsy, there was a big, orange NPO sign on the door. NPO is Latin for "nothing by mouth". It's unusual to see Trey in a lot of pain. He's always been the child that never complained. If he did, something was wrong. As a matter of fact, he pushed himself so much in football, just prior to hospitalization, that we have no idea when this started. He complained a little about not being able to run full out or being out of breath, but not anything major. He would chalk it up to being tired and go to bed. Trying to reduce his oral pain medication didn't work. Soon, he was back to the stronger IV pain medication. Dilaudid is his friend.

Dr. Alberto Pappo, the head of the solid tumors, told us this morning they were still unsure of what was going on and would not let us leave until they were sure. Dr. Pappo's hugs were something I welcomed each time I saw him. They also promised to make sure his pain was under control. That was reassuring to me. I didn't want to take Trey home and not be able to ease his pain.

During Trey's birth, I hemorrhaged and was bedridden, unable to care for him, for weeks. Now, I found myself reliving those feelings. Would I be able to care for him now?

While I was thinking through the logistics of having him home, he mumbled, "Where's the medicine!" At least, now, he can talk.

The hospital stay has been a parade of doctors and things I cannot remember. It's so unbelievably frustrating. I'd love to get all the doctors in one room and ask them to speak very slowly and in English, not medical terms! Two doctors want to do a scope to biopsy the pancreas, but one is at Methodist and one is at Baptist. St. Jude does not do this procedure. I didn't know there was anything St. Jude didn't do!

Despite the bright colors in the hallways and the smiles from people I don't know, I have a feeling something bad is coming. Call it a mother's intuition!

The walk to and from the cafeteria seems like a mile. Jay and I take turns going to get something to eat and make ourselves leave Trey's side. Trey actually tells us to go. I'm glad Jay has an appetite and is able to eat. I think nerves have the best of my stomach. But I am thankful for the Starbuck's!

We received more disappointing news from the liver scan. Remember the feeling I had when I thought something bad was coming? The spots on Trey's liver were originally thought to behemangiomas, a collection of blood vessels. After the scan, they say they don't know what it is. So, it looks like he'll either have a liver biopsy or a PET scan to see if he lights up for cancer.

Even with the uncertainty surrounding a diagnosis, we still believe we are in the best place. We still believe we God is on his throne. We still believe in miracles and still believe God has a plan. And we are still strong in our faith. Just because we are tired, but in our weakness, God is ever present working in our lives.

Our room at St. Jude feels a little bit like a press briefing room. Nurses constantly run in and out with different information. Now, we've been told Trey will have a PET scan tomorrow to see where he lights up for cancer. The pancreas will light up because of the activity going on there, but this will also tell us what is going on in the liver. We are praying for clarity.

I've been receiving so many emails and telephone calls questioning if we are doing the right thing with our treatment choices. How do you ever know if you are doing the right thing? A week ago, our son was on the football field practicing with his teammates. Last weekend, he was praising the Lord and worshipping during DNOW at Germantown Baptist Church. Today, we are waiting for a definitive diagnosis to get down to what is wrong with Trey. *"Trust in the Lord with all your heart and lean not to your own understanding. In all your ways acknowledge Him and He will direct your path."* Proverbs 3:5-6

At this point, the only thing we know for sure is we are not going home any time soon. Trey is not in physical shape to go home. He cannot tolerate any kind of food, not even pudding. When he does go home, he MAY have to go home with a PICC line to feed him liquids because he cannot eat solids. Just think, the pancreas, the size of a thumb, is causing all of this in his body. That's so HARD to imagine!

He's lost approximately 12 pounds over the last couple of weeks. They weigh him every morning. Some mornings, when I see the pain on his face as he gets of bed, I want to ask the nurses to wait until later. When he entered St. Jude, he weighed 150 pounds, something he worked hard to get to. The weight loss bothers him the most. To top off the weight loss, he's jaundice.

We are thankful he didn't go home until they have a definite treatment plan in place; and he can't tolerate oral pain medicine to manage the pain. Even though he's a strong kid, he can't manage anything right now and it frustrates him to feel dependent. If you ask to help him, stand back because he will tell you he can do it.

Trey read Jesus Calling and said, "Hey Mom, you know what the verse was for today? Philippians 4:6 "Be anxious for nothing...".

Comments like that make me wonder who is supposed to be encouraging whom?

Collin is home sick and cannot come stay at the hospital. We miss him, even though he loves being with his Aunt Donna. Trey is more worried about Collin than anyone. He just wants him to come to the hospital and sit.

While we have had lots of visitors, the front desk rarely calls. One day, Jay received a call and talked for several minutes before handing the phone to Trey. Trey's face lit up when he realized Josh Pastner, Coach of the Memphis Tigers, was on the other end.

Soon, Jay's phone rang again. I heard him say D. J. and our room number. I realized D. J. Stephens, Trey's favorite University of Memphis Basketball player was on his way up to our room. Trey had always been an avid U of M Basketball fan and had tweeted at D. J. numerous times. What we didn't know was Coach Pastner asked D. J. to come see Trey at the hospital. Realizing he was on the way, I looked around the room and thought OH NO! The room is covered in University of Tennessee! We happen to be a house divided and love the University of Tennessee also. Trey even has on a UT t-shirt.

After he got off the phone with Coach Pastner, we made him change t-shirts, threw all the orange things in the closet, tossed his UT blanket in the bathtub, and he jumped in bed like nothing had been going on. Trey has been a UT Vol fan since a small child. Trey's energy level went from a zero to 10 when D. J. and his girlfriend, Stacie, came in the room. It is amazing what one person can do. We laughed and laughed, all out of breath! It didn't take long before Trey and D. J. were hamming it up, taking pictures, making bets, and planning for Trey to attend an upcoming game. D. J. and Coach are working it out for us to go to the conference game. Later, Trey tweeted *"Had an awesome day thanks to @DdotJAY30 thanks for comin homie."* And the picture pose was set!

CHAPTER 4

SCARY TESTS AND MEDICINE

"With all prayer and petition pray at all times in the Spirit, and with this in view, be on the alert with all perseverance and petition for all the saints…" Ephesians 6:18

March 2, 2012

We were still waiting for the scan results when a reporter from Channel 5 news called and asked to meet us off campus. Honestly, it felt good to get out and drive down the street. We only got around the corner before my cell phone rang. Dr. Pappo was on the line and he asked we return to the hospital right away. He didn't tell us why. Jay and I didn't say a word. I felt like all the blood was draining from me, like I was out of my body sitting next to myself. God put a choir song in my head and I kept repeating, "You deserve the Glory and The Honor."

When we arrived back at the hospital, Dr. Sara and Dr. Pappo came in to tell us about the PET scan. It showed several hot spots in the liver and one in the pancreas. They will do a biopsy on Monday, March 5. The results from the blood work showed Trey had elevated tumor markers, possibly due to pancreatitis. We tried to see the bright side. Maybe these counts were related to pancreatitis and nothing else!

Trey will be transported by ambulance on Tuesday to Methodist Central for an ERCP scope to scrape his pancreas for cancer. Basically, this test is like an endoscopy, with the addition of a camera and an ultrasound. After the test, he was to return to to St. Jude to wait for results from both the biopsy of the liver and the pancreas scrape.

Everything came so fast. We weren't given the chance to say no. Not that we would, but what if we had wanted to question what was being done to Trey? We are trusting in the doctors at St. Jude.

Trey received a PICC line in his arm today to receive nutrients. He thinks it is cool. I think he would not think it was so cool if he didn't have the pain medications. He is still not able to eat. He is so hungry! Please pray for him in that regard! He needs strength. He will not be able to eat until next week. Well, he will TRY to eat next week. After the procedure, Trey tweeted (with a photo) *"Got a PICC line today connected to my heart."* He also got a Dilaudid pain pump today! With some things, the doctors and nurses move quickly. With others, they seem to move so slowly. I guess it is all in our perception. We have known he has needed the pain pump for days. He is using the pain pump regularly and I'm glad he's not afraid to use it. His pain has increased each day. Trey sleeps curled up in the fetal position when he is in pain. The doctors have asked us to be patient, but when your child is hurting, you want to do whatever you can to take pain away and fix the problem. This is one problem we cannot fix until we know exactly what is going on.

God's hand is so evident. We had a precious doctor pray with us today. She was so touched by our faith and felt led to pray for us. I was so blessed. I have never had a doctor acknowledge their faith, let alone pray with me. We have experienced many things, so different from what I feel we would experience at just any hospital. God is in this room. God is at St. Jude.

As I try to get comfortable in the extended couch/bed I sleep in each night, my prayers always go back to Collin. My other baby has the flu and I miss him. I know his Aunt Donna is taking good care of him. I have also been told they are working on t-shirts and when I know more, I'll let you know. The outpouring of love for our family is overwhelming. Keep up the trend! #prayfortrey

March 3, 2012

"I worship the one who is Jesus. I worship the one who is born the Son of God."

Trey has had a very restful day and we are very thankful. Maybe his pain pump and nausea medications are at the right levels. Trey has needed a day of not having to be poked and prodded. He's too tired to tweet, but his phone never leaves his hand or the side of his head. He also has his bible and his devotion book close by.

We received his counts this morning and his lipase is down to 1,055. This is such good news. We are hoping his not eating is calming his pancreas down. Remember, it has been as high as 4,000 and the norm is 100.

He started his TPN (Total Parenteral Nourishment) last night. This is a bag of nutrients he receives through his line to bypass his digestive system. Unfortunately, it made him nauseated last night when he went to bed. When he woke this morning, he was even more nauseated. He has had a bad case of hiccups since he woke up with his nausea and it has caused him to begin throwing up. Not a good start to the morning, but more nausea medications on board! He has tolerated his TPN all day with the help of his nausea medications. We laughed when we first received the TPN. It looks like a huge bag of Gatorade. The doctors told us this would help him gain strength and put a little weight back on. We'll take anything at this point.

We received his bilirubin counts and they have gone up to 4.5. The norm should be 1.0. His eyes are more yellow this morning. He also started itching on his legs. They told us this is all due to his liver counts. Trey will not stop scratching his legs so they brought Benadryl.

After watching the Memphis basketball game, Julianne, Trey's girlfriend, Jay and I decided to get Trey OUT of the hospital. We rolled Trey to the gift shop. We stayed out for about 30 minutes before Trey was not feeling well and we had to return to the room. He's very weak from just being in the bed for so many days. I still think the fresh air did him some good. Nausea is a powerful player in this game. Trey fights it every second.

We are SO thankful for the pain pump. This has helped him so much! It has been a basketball watching kind of day! We are praying for a peaceful night's sleep for us all. We know tomorrow's counts can be different just with the touch of God's hand.

#prayfortrey

March 4, 2012

Trey is now receiving a continuous dose of Dilaudid through his line and is able to push his pump. After analyzing how much he pushed his pump within 24 hours, the pump was adjusted so he could get the medication more frequently. The change in the pain medication has seemed to help.

We had more trouble today with the hiccups. His oncologist, Dr. Sara Federico called today to check on him and said the hiccups could be caused from an aggravated diaphragm. NOT good when he's nauseated too.

Pain medication also causes constipation so Trey hasn't been able to go to the bathroom in a couple of days. When he was first admitted to St. Jude, the nurse asked him what he usually called going to the bathroom so the nurses and doctors could talk on his level. We all looked at each other not knowing exactly what would come out of Trey's mouth.

"Well, taking a dump," he answered.

We all cracked up laughing because that is Trey. The nurses have been asking him repeatedly if he has taken a dump. Today, we started watching the bathroom scene from the movie "Dumb and Dumber" just for laughs. Trey never went to the bathroom, but we sure did laugh a lot, over and over.

Trey also had a good visit with Aunt Donna and Uncle Bill. He enjoyed showing Aunt Donna all his lines and his feeding tube (TPN) which he thinks is "cool". At least that's what he wants Aunt Donna to think! I was a little hesitant about their visit because Collin had been sick. However, upon entering and leaving the hospital, all visitors have to scrub and disinfect. If there is a germ alive, I would be surprised. It was good for Donna to see Trey and hear him say "Love you Aunt Donna" when she left the room. Occasionally, she could see the look of pain on his face and he would take a deep breath and close his eyes. For the most part, though, he was his funny self.

Donna has an anatomy book at home, so, as we have received new information or Trey has a new procedure scheduled, she has explained it to Collin. The last thing we want to do is keep Collin in the dark. When Jay goes home to get a change of clothes, he knows there will be no doubts with Collin. I still have not been home to spend time with Collin.

Trey was able to grab a date with a nurse, Pam! She made him walk to the nurse's station for his medicine and then walk with her around the hall a little. When he returned to the room, I asked him where he was going.

"Let's go," he said. "I'm going to make another circle."

The second circle wore him out. I believe knowing he could accomplish one more circle around the nurse's station was very good for him mentally and emotionally.

What he couldn't see was me behind him in tears as he said, "Come on Mama!"

We covet your prayers for tomorrow's biopsy of the liver. We are scheduled to head down at 7:30 a.m. and Dr. Gold will be doing the biopsy at St. Jude. We specifically ask they will find nothing. Whatever they biopsy will BE nothing. Selfishly, we ask we will receive the results accurately and quickly. We are praying Trey will not experience much pain after the biopsy. We have been told the liver tends to bleed and that is the last thing we need. I think they scare you on purpose so you will be prepared if something happens.

We have such an awesome Collierville Dragon family. Coach Mike O'Neill visited today and brought Trey a basketball signed by the University of Memphis Tigers team while under Coach Calipari. It was given to Coach O'Neill to give to Trey by a boy who had it in a collection. More importantly, he gave Trey a wooden cross to wear around his neck. The bond between coach and player is so important and to see Trey's varsity football coach reach out with such compassion is heartwarming. Trey misses his teammates and knowing they are preparing for spring practice is on his mind. It gives him more determination to get well. Coach O'Neill and I even had a conversation in the hall about what kind of equipment could be provided to protect his pancreas when he returns in the fall. Trey is determined to get back on the field and we have only been dealing with this situation for a week or more!

Jay and I have been told there are more Pray For Trey t-shirts available. I think they sell out as soon as they get them in. I know Sonya Luna and Lynne Berry have been working hard to get the orders filled. Who would have ever thought such a thing would have caught on so fast, like wildfire? What a blessing it is to feel the support from the

Collierville community, knowing they are wearing t-shirts asking others to pray for Trey during this time. It keeps coming to my mind some of the kids buying the shirts may not normally pray. What is God teaching them? I pray God is touching hearts by spreading the word of praying for Trey.

I loved the scripture Trey tweeted today. He knows tomorrow will be a big day. "Be joyful; pray continually; give thanks in all circumstances, for it is God's will for you in Christ Jesus." 1 Thessalonians 5:16-18. Trey and I were talking about scripture tonight and how some scripture means different things to different people. The scripture he's claiming during this journey is James 1:2-3:

> "Consider it pure joy, my brethren, when you
> encounter various trials, knowing that the testing
> of your faith produces endurance."

I am cherishing the precious time with my boy at night before bedtime as he nods off to what he is calling la la land. Sleep my precious boy.

March 5, 2012

Jay and I sat patiently in a holding room while Trey was having his biopsy. I was thankful they allowed us to go with him to the procedure room and stay with him as they put him to sleep. Emotionally, it was almost more than Jay and I could handle. I have a fear of being put to sleep so watching the sodium penathol slowly go into his line made my knees weak. The room started to spin. I felt blood rush quickly all threw my body, and my throat sink into my stomach while thinking, "I can't pass out here!" Trey was in pain so he never opened his eyes. Maybe he was afraid. I kissed his hand over and over and told him this was the kind of sleep I liked! His scanner had Buzz Lightyear and Woody on it. I wanted to take a picture because Buzz was one of his favorite characters. When I told him Buzz was there, he turned and gave me one of those teenager looks! It brought to mind the picture I took of him on the table in the pediatrician's office with Buzz over his head just a few days before we ended up in the hospital.

Our prayers are two-fold. We pray they will get a good biopsy (if the Lord sees fit for anything to be there) and THERE WILL BE NO RESIDUAL BLEEDING. It's such a risk. Because of the precarious place of the biopsy, he was scheduled for a scan this afternoon to look for bleeding from the liver. The largest spot is under the capsule of the liver and hard to reach by interventional biopsy. Sometimes, I ask myself what was going on and wonder if this is real. The other way to monitor bleeding is through blood levels. Luckily, he has his PICC line so they don't have to stick him to get samples. We were told he would be uncomfortable after the procedure. Actually, it took more time to measure, find the place in the liver, etc. than to perform the actual biopsy. There is also a chance the doctor will stop the procedure if it seems unsafe. This test is very important in determining what is going on with his liver and pancreas. Even in the best scenario, we won't receive results for a couple of days. The running joke between the three of us has been when someone said it would be an hour, they really meant three hours. So, when they say a couple of days, it probably means a week.

The Lord spoke this to me today...

"For the earth will be filled with the knowledge of the glory of the Lord as the waters cover the sea."
Habakkuk 2:14.

Amen and Amen.

We were waiting for Trey when he came into recovery. Obviously, Trey and anesthesia don't mix, hence throwing up. While Trey was sitting up, I took out my phone and began to take pictures of his back.

"What are you doing," asked Jay?

"Taking a picture," I answered. "Trey will want to know what his back looked like."

About that time, Trey said, "Mom, what does it look like? Take pictures." I cut my eyes at Jay and grinned.

Trey did great during the biopsy. The doctor said when he removed the needle there was not one drop of blood! Thank you, Lord! Dr. Gold got three biopsies of one spot, about 1 1/2 centimeters. THAT'S SMALL! They got enough for the pathologist to give us a good diagnosis, although not quickly. We still have to wait a couple of days. God provided the most amazing doctors. They pray with us, they hug us, they cry with me, and our main oncologist just gave Trey and I pocket angels to hold.

There are so many little prayers and so many answers. One thing I do know: no prayer for God is too small. I cannot tell you how awesome the doctors were. We are holding on to God's promises that He will not forsake us or leave us. And we know St. Jude feels the same way.

We were told the test at Methodist, scheduled for tomorrow, might be postponed so we were left to pray over the pathologist and the biopsy results. We didn't know if God was preparing us FOR something or if He had already taken us through it. Either way, we are desperately seeking and trusting Him.

It has been a long day for Trey. He has been in a lot of pain, mostly from his pancreas, not from the biopsy site. They increased his pain medications again. I've lost count of how many times they have done that but Trey is keeping a tally of how many things he has things done! It's kind of amusing.

Things have changed. Our trip to Methodist changed because Dr. Ismail feels it is important to receive the results of the liver biopsy before doing anything to the pancreas.

Dr. Ismail's plans for the pancreas, at this point, are to do an ERCP (scope) on Wednesday, ultrasound, possible biopsy, and put in a stent. Our heads are spinning today. We acknowledge Satan attacked us when we were weak to break us down and make us doubt by the way we were spoken to this afternoon. That's all I'm going to say about that. But I am not going to let Satan get credit.

We'll get the results of the liver biopsy tomorrow. We will gather with the doctors around noon to discuss the results. Dr. Pappo put a rush on the pathologist and got things done.

We KNOW God has the pathologist results in HIS hands. We KNOW He can wipe it clean. We KNOW God hears all things, knows all things, and controls all things. Please pray it is His will for Trey to be healed. Pray this pathology report comes back loud and clear to be clean of cancer and something so amazing to the doctors they cannot explain how, except by the hands of God. There are believers here at St. Jude. This can be something he has had for years and benign. Pray whatever is in pancreas will be healed by a simple procedure and Trey will recover quickly.

We call out to you, Lord Jesus.

We are nothing special. We are not an inspiration. We are just a mom and a dad begging God for their child's life. We ask that you help us on our behalf as we become weary and confused by the things we hear from day to day and "maybes" become reality.

My friend Hollee says, "I think I'll go to bed listening to my Jesus music." I cannot do it. Trey listens to his music all day and night, to tune everyone out and cope. If I put my Jesus music on, I think I would fall apart. It's very hard at night. Trey is trying to sleep and the nurses are doing what they need to do. My brain is reeling from everything we have been told the last couple of days. Then come the "what if?" questions. I have to stop myself from going to that place and begin to pray. I pray for God to protect Trey, heal him and that we will wake up in our own beds. Somehow, God gives just the measure of strength we need. Jay and I have not been eating in front of Trey and I have not been eating much at all. God has protected me from a migraine. Jay says it is because of the filtered oxygen. As I fall asleep tonight, I sing to myself and pray over my child.

CHAPTER 5

DIAGNOSIS

"And we know that God causes all things to work together for good to those who love God, to those who are called according to His purpose." Romans 8:28

March 6, 2012

We're here all morning before the conference with the doctors at 1 p.m. Our Youth Minister, Keith Cochran, and our Music Minister, Ron Norton, came to be with us. Jay's mother, Cecelia, was also with us. We tried making jokes, but nothing seems funny. No one wants to eat. The hours pass so slowly and the clock never moves. Occasionally, I got up from my little hole in the corner I had made for myself and paced back and forth to and from the nurse's station. My little cuddle corner gives me comfort. From there, I can see Trey and reach him in two seconds. When we sleep, I can watch him. Most nights I do. It's where all Trey's lab reports, my computer, my Ipad, my St. Jude binder, and various leftover drinks brought by sweet friends are stacked

Dr. Sara and Karen Williams finally came to take Jay, his mother and I to a small conference room. Keith and Ron stayed with Trey as we talked with the doctor. One of our favorite nurses, Judy, and another doctor were also with us in a very small conference room. Everyone sat but Jay, who leaned up against the wall behind the door.

Immediately, Dr. Sara said, "I cannot believe I am telling you this, but Trey has been diagnosed with pancreatic adenocarcinoma and it has spread to his liver, stage 4.

This is the adult kind of cancer. There is not a cure and it would be a miracle if he was cured."

I was in such shock. She was talking about someone else's child, not mine. There was a mix up. I looked at Jay to question him and to see if I was hearing it correctly? Thankfully, Cecelia was there and she asked about the prognosis. Dr. Sara said he had been given 3-5 months without treatment and 11 months with treatment. I couldn't breathe. I lost it. Jay lost it. Dr. Sara was crying. How could this adult disease attack a 15 year old child? I wanted answers and I wanted them immediately!

The answers Dr. Sara was giving were not making sense. They seemed to be going in my head and swishing around like in a fish bowl. The meeting lasted an hour. We had so much discussion yet, I couldn't recall anything to explain to Trey. All I could remember was 11 months with treatment and helping him have quality of life. Quality of life? Like he has had the last week? Is this real? I just know someone else was going through this. Not me. Not us.

How were we going to tell Trey, tell Collin? Dr. Sara said she would be happy to tell Trey. When we walked in the room, Trey saw I had been crying and said, "Oh, it must be bad, Mom's been crying." I just curled up in the bed behind him so he would not see me cry when Dr. Sara told him. The room was full of people – nurses, doctors, friends. She had such simple, compassionate words, and didn't make it a drawn out explanation. She told him she didn't know what God had planned. Trey already knew. He was prepared. God had prepared him. She asked him if he understood.

"I'll be okay," he said. "I'll either be healthy here, or I'll be healthy in heaven."

We all gave a big sigh to his explanation of the diagnosis he had received for his future. His next tweet was,

"Hakuna Matata." This means "no worries" and it was from his favorite Disney movie, "The Lion King".

For hours, Jay and I walked around in a daze, trying to be upbeat. Our phones have been going nuts with love and prayers. Bobby, my nephew, spent so much time at the hospital. He and I sat and, jokingly, watched the numbers go up on my phone inbox. Sometimes, you have to find humor in the little things.

Trey's attitude was good but he was not very talkative or texting much. I remember writing that night, "The battle is not over. Your prayers are still needed. All of the doctors have been wonderful and are amazed at our extraordinary son, Trey. God created him for a purpose."

How will any of us sleep? I cannot sleep. Who's going to tell my mother? I prayed "one day at a time, sweet Jesus. That's all we're asking from you."
#prayfortrey

> **Julianne Shiles' Thoughts:** I remember when I first heard Trey had cancer. I told myself he would get better and this would be over. I didn't know how to fix it because Trey always fixed things. I was scared for both of us. Cody Jordan, Madison Young and I always drove together to the hospital to see Trey. I knew I couldn't do it alone. I just felt lost.

> **Madison Luna's Thoughts:** I remember the day I was told Trey had been diagnosed with Pancreatic Cancer. I walked upstairs and my mom was in my brother's room crying. She told me the news and I was shocked. I had known Trey since elementary school. There

was no way someone my age could be diagnosed with an adult disease. We cried together and tried to think of ways to help, but only God could do that. Trey was someone dear to our hearts, and it was so hard to watch my friend go from a strong football player, to someone smaller than me. However, Trey showed no signs of fear because he knew that God was taking care of him and His will was being done. His first tweet after being diagnosed was "Hakuna Matata," which means no worries. Wow. Even in that first instant, when the news was fresh, Trey had comfort in God. He lost his physical strength, but he never lost his stronghold in the Lord. He never questioned God once. He inspired me, along with so many others, to learn more about having a close relationship with the Lord like he did. I tried to think of how I would react in his situation. Would I have the faith he had? I don't know if I would have, but Trey made me stronger. How, you might ask, could someone with a deadly illness like cancer make a healthy person stronger? By living like Jesus.

March 7, 2012

Trey's first tweet of the day was, *"Gonna be a rough day."* His next tweet was *"God will never give you more than what you can handle."* Trey has his priorities straight and knows where to put his faith, even on rough days. Who raised this kid?

After receiving the news yesterday, no time was wasted in beginning to treat Trey and relieve his pain. That's how St. Jude rolls. We have the best team of doctors in Dr. Pappo and Dr. Federico. The sad thing is we have to leave this wonderful place. We feel safe here.

Since Trey has an adult disease, he also needs to be treated by an adult oncologist. Dr. Sara came in and told us she made a call to West Clinic. She spoke to a doctor and after giving him the history, the doctor asked the name of the patient. She told him and he said, "Oh, of course I'll take him."

Dr. Sara didn't know the doctor she was talking to, Dr. Kurt Tauer, was Jay's doctor and had been Jay's brother's doctor before he passed away. She came to tell us she had spoken to a doctor at West Clinic. The day had been moving so fast and we didn't have time to think about any choices of where to go for adult consult or treatment. When she said she had talked with Dr. Kurt Tauer, I just grinned. She said, "What?"

We had to tell her our history and current status with Dr. Tauer and she already knew. Dr. Tauer had told her. God intervenes just when you need Him to step in and show you He is in control. Many people don't understand why we have chosen to stay with St. Jude. We have received very rude and threatening emails and phone calls, mostly to tell us we are idiots and THEY can heal our son. With water? Seriously? Sometimes, I don't even get the chance to ask how they got our phone number.

We are to see Kurt Tauer on Friday at 9 a.m. We will either be seeing him at West Clinic or at Methodist Germantown. Right now, we are not sure what the plan for leaving St. Jude will be. We've been told it all depends on Trey. Remember, this is very rare to have at his age. We contacted MD Anderson and they told us the youngest patient they had treated with pancreatic cancer was in their 20's. Even though Trey is not eligible for any clinical trials, I wonder why other hospitals have not been jumping at the chance to treat something so rare. We are definitely not giving up. We are contacting centers all over the country. There has to be information they can give St. Jude or West Clinic.

Trey had to be transported to Methodist Central today to have an ERCP, an Endoscopic Retrograde Cholangio-Pancreatogaphy. This test involves a scope that will examine Trey's liver, bile duct, and pancreas. We have been told this test can be very dangerous to the pancreas and can cause pancreatitis. Sometimes they scrape the pancreas to get a biopsy. At this point, Jay, Trey, and I feel there's nothing to lose. He already has pancreatitis!

When we arrived at Methodist Central, Jay and I ran into a friend, Scott Green, waiting for Trey to go into the operating room. Everyone had on scrub hats that said *PrayForTrey.* We were in awe. Everywhere we turned, someone we didn't know had a scrub hat on their head that said the same thing. It was like being in an insurance commercial. Trey was in pain and didn't seem as phased by the hats as we were. Even though we had experienced being with Trey before his other tests, I felt helpless when they took him away from me to go into the operating room. All I could do was stand in the doorway and look at all the machines around him. As strong as he was trying to be through his pain, I knew he was scared. This test was going to tell us so much; exactly where the cancer was located in the pancreas and to what degree. There were nurses were nice enough to say they would take care of him. Trey was very quiet.

It seemed like Jay, Cindy Few and I waited all day. The doctor came and told us the ERCP was very successful.

There had been a chance they would not be able to insert the stent. Once they got in, they were able to insert a metal stent in his bile duct which was obstructed. They said everything began to flow from the pancreas immediately. This will help his pain AND his jaundice. They did find several ulcerations which were biopsied. They suspect these are malignant.

The first thing Trey said when he got into the room at Methodist was he had to go to the bathroom. Even after having a serious medical procedure, he was still determined to do everything on his own. That didn't work out quite like he wanted and we were able to get a good laugh at his expense as his slid down the wall of the bathroom in his gown.

We originally thought we were on the schedule for Trey to have a nerve block on his pancreas on Thursday. This would make him feel so much better. We decided, however, it would be best for Trey to begin to feel better before this procedure. Trey became very upset before the procedure when he found out he would not be put to sleep for the nerve block. There is no reason to upset him now.

First and foremost, we want to get him to the University of Memphis basketball game tomorrow night. He has been talking about the game since D. J. Stephens offered the tickets. Those are the things that matter now. So many are asking how we are doing. We are tired - emotionally, mentally, and physically. We have not alternated nights and we needed to. We are just not going to leave our boy. We promised him from the beginning we would not leave him. We are told one thing will happen one day and, as I have said before, it changes like a revolving door. So there will be no leaving him.

Away from the hospital, we are amazed at the things that are being done for our family, sometimes without our knowledge. Our Collierville High School family is amazing! We just hope someone will save us #prayfortrey t-shirts. We have been told there is a white t-shirt with Pray For Trey on the front and the scripture from Philippians 4:13 "I can do all things who strengthens me." on the back. I also heard the Health Sciences class was selling blue Pray For Trey t-shirts. There are t-shirts that have been SOLD OUT. Bracelets have been sold and given out. Even the Collierville High School football team worked on our yard today. How wonderful to serve one of their own! Let HIS light shine Collierville! We will need you when we get home and he CAN eat! And will need to catch up on SCHOOL!

Trey even received a shout out from the Pete Pranica, the Memphis Grizzlies announcer before a game - IN CALIFORNIA! GOD IS ALL OVER THIS! I cannot even begin to tell you what the Memphis Fire Department friends are doing for Jay. They are covering his shifts through April. How can we say thank you? We cannot; we are so humbled. These are blessings that happen to others, not us. God has been good by putting just the right people in our path. We will continue to pray for this.

The best way I can explain what we are going through is God does not select weak people to do His work. He chooses the strong. That's why Trey and our family have been chosen. That's not to say there won't be rough, emotional days. We are human. But as Trey told the doctor yesterday, "I'll either be healthy here, or healthy in heaven."

I think back to February 9. Trey had a bad headache at school that day. He sent me a text because he didn't know how to check out of school. I remember sitting at work almost irritated at his ignorance.

"Just go to the office and tell them your Dad is picking you up," I replied.

"Ok," he said, "so I go to the nurse and call?"
"YES!", I answered.

A few days later, Trey and I laughed at how he didn't know how to check out of school. Trey is never sick and I should have picked up on something. Especially since he wanted to leave school and miss football practice. That was just not his character. I didn't know, then, severe headaches are a symptom of pancreatic cancer.

My mind is going in millions of directions and it seems St. Jude has an answer for everything. We will need so much help when we get home. Trey wants to go back to school, bless his heart. There are so many things to consider when you go back to school - schoolwork load, doctor's appointments, GERMS! We are not sure this will happen, but Karen Williams, our Quality of Life coordinator, is trying to coordinate as many things as she can for him, including a Make a Wish trip.

Make a Wish is another thing that "other" people plan. It's not for our family, not for Trey. I didn't know you don't have to be terminal to take a Make a Wish trip. Make a Wish can grant a wish to anyone they approve.

We still plead for your continued prayers. Trey needs strength and has not eaten in many days. He is losing strength very fast and wanting to sleep. We know it will take a lot of nourishment to get him moving around. It is very easy to lie in bed, make plans to go home and return to school. It is another thing to get out of bed and walk down the hall.

March 8, 2012

Trey tweeted *"Then have no care for tomorrow; tomorrow will take care of itself. Take the trouble of the day as it comes. Matthew 6:34 #noworries"*. It's another day I ask myself if he knows something I don't.

There are days I ask myself, "Why did God send this person to visit on THIS day? I know Katy asked herself many questions after she lost her husband to cancer only after a month or so after his diagnosis. Katy and I have been friends since we were children. Katy and her father came to visit Trey and it was a total surprise. Not only did she bring puzzle books, magazines, and note cards, but she shared an idea already had in the works. She was in the process of setting up an account at BankTennessee for Trey in the name, **Friends of Trey Erwin**. Jay and I cannot even wrap our minds around it. So, we take advice from others who have walked down this road and tell us there will be expenses and we will need help along the way. Techinically, St. Jude is paying for everything. But there are so many other incidentals that are not covered and we don't know what will come our way down the road. I cannot imagine walking into a bank branch and seeing my son's face on a **Friends of Trey Erwin** can or flyer. It has nothing to do with pride. It just makes the entire situation a little more real.

Today, we had a lot of doctors checking on Trey after his procedure yesterday. Because it was so late in the day, he slept all late afternoon and evening, but didn't sleep last night, even with good drugs. The side effects of the procedure hit today, including major nausea. We tried a couple of things to alleviate the nausea, but that just caused more vomiting. I don't think there is anything left for him to throw up. His strength is gone. I am learning how to convert St. Jude's weight measurements into pounds and his body is definitely beginning to reflect the weight loss. Each day, he's down a pound here or there. After five or six days, he's down over 13 pounds. He had already begun to lose when he came into the hospital. Taking a shower wiped him out.

When it was time to get ready for the University of Memphis basketball game, he was wavering about whether to go. We told him we would take him as far as he felt he could go. So we bundled him up and got him as far as the lobby of the Forum when he said he could not make it. He was shivering uncontrollably so we turned around and came back to St. Jude. We made the best decision. We know Trey was disappointed.

Tomorrow we head to West Clinic. There might be a long wait and it will take everything Trey has to make it through the day. Please pray for his strength. I am not so sure he is looking forward to leaving St. Jude. I am not looking forward to leaving either. We love the nurses and the doctors and get such good personal care. I will be honest. I am scared of leaving St. Jude. There are so many medications Trey takes at different times and, if he misses just one dose, he can become violently ill. He has to take three to four Pancrealipace at least 10 minutes before he eats a snack. Then, when he eats a meal, he has to take five Pancrealipace and wait 10 minutes. That goes along with his Zofran, Phenergan, Phenergan gel, Ativan, Benedryl, and Scopolomine patch for nausea. He's also taking Docusate-Senna for his intestines, Levaquin, an antibiotic, Pantoprazole for reflux, Polyethylene glycol 3350, better known as MiraLAX, Morphine, Tylenol, Compazine suppositories, Dexamethasone (steroid). Additionally, we have all the supplies for his Dilaudid pain pump and his TPN feeding line. This doesn't include the chemotherapy drugs. It's just what we are going to administer at home. Our trust and faith is totally in God that He will take care of us at home. We know Trey will thrive better at home.

Keith Cochran told me he had received several calls from people asking how they can help our family. We are honored. Please pray for us as we have many decisions to make. Trey has to make his Make a Wish decision. We have insurance issues, financial assistance issues, work issues, and sibling issues, all while trying to keep things normal as we go home tomorrow. And he wants to go back to school! Oh my!

He asked me tonight if he really had 11 months to live. I told him God is faithful; we need to keep trusting in God and not doubt. God's plan is perfect and we don't know what it is.

"Are you scared?", I asked.

"No," he answered

I'm glad he doesn't know how much his mama is sometimes!

CHAPTER 6

WEST CLINIC - OUR FIRST DAY

"Pray for anything and if you have faith, you will receive it."
Matthew 21:22

March 10, 2012

After we checked out of St. Jude yesterday morning, we headed to West Clinic for our 9 a.m. appointment. West Clinic was expecting us and there was no wait whatsoever. What a blessing!

We saw Dr. Tauer and made the decision to start a chemotherapy regimen called F5U. His chemotherapy consists of Fluoroucil (F5U) to treat pancreatic cancer and also stop or slow the growth of cancer cells, Oxaliplatin, an alkylating agent used to slow or stop the growth of the cancer cells, Leucovorin, an intravenous vitamin, and Irinotecan, a cancer patient favorite. Not all of these medications can be run at the same time. The F5U was to be given by injection into a line. It only takes three to five minutes to run while the Oxaliplatin and Irinotecan run intravenously for, at least, two hours. While Irinotecan can cause horrible diarrhea, Oxaliplatin causes severe sensitivity to cold.

He will receive his first chemotherapy treatment on Monday at West Clinic. The next two days he will receive it through his IV pump at home. He will go back in two weeks to receive another treatment and so on. These will be very long days. Dr. Tauer says if Trey starts feeling better, they will know the treatment is working. Of course, they will do scans, but the first indication will be he is feeling better. The main side effects are diarrhea and mouth sores. Dr. Tauer does not think he will lose much of his hair. If he does, it will begin after the first two weeks of treatment. Many of the side effects of the treatment Trey is receiving can be treated with medication. Most adults tolerate it well.

Dr. Tauer was concerned about how lethargic Trey seemed. He asked if he was always this tired or did he have times he was more alert. We told him there were times he was more alert and attributed his lethargy to his pain medication. Dr. Tauer began to explain what he had already put in place for the day, hoping Trey would agree with the procedure - a nerve block on his pancreas. He also wanted to remove his PICC line and replace it with a Hickman line to be used for his chemotherapy. Dr. Tauer told us the same things we had been told before. Trey is a 15 year old with a 60 year old man's disease. He has an athletic, healthy body and we are going to approach this in a positive manner. Dr. Tauer told us all the side effects of the different drugs. The biggest side effects are diarrhea, mouth sores, and nausea.

Dr. Tauer asked Trey, "Are you ready to do this?"

"Yes sir," Trey answered.

At West Clinic, the first procedure was a nerve block on his pancreas.This was a very long procedure, but it had to be in exactly the right place in order to block the nerve for the pancreas. Like Dr. Tauer explained to Trey before the procedure, the good thing about this block is there is no mistaking where Dr. Hodgkiss needed to go with his needles. He had scans to tell him exactly where to go. We tried to ease Trey's nerves by comparing them to the epidural blocks I have had for my back. There was only a slight possibility the procedure would not be successful. As I held Trey's hand during the procedure, I just prayed and prayed he would get the right spot. I have had blocks before and know the importance of not moving during the procedure. Trey wanted to see the screen during the procedure and I tried to take pictures for him. Luckily for Trey, the block worked perfectly. After the block, Trey announced he was pain free.

Later, they removed his PICC line and put in a Hickman line on the left side of his chest just below his collarbone. He cannot swim with this, but it can be converted to a portacath easily. Trey is okay with this because, right now, he's leaning toward a trip to Hawaii through Make a Wish! I don't think Collin will complain! His second wish is Orlando. Once again, we're blessed to know the volunteer helping us with Make a Wish. Small world? I think not.

We left with a lot of promising information for the future from Dr. Tauer. He's not giving up! After chemotherapy, the tumor in his pancreas could get to the point it could be shrunk by other methods. Dr. Tauer also mentioned the liver lesions could be removed with a microwave like probe and, hopefully, stop them from spreading. All of these suggestions sound wonderful, but they will only come into the picture when Trey has endured the chemotherapy and is strong enough to handle additional procedures.

It's very important for people to know why Jay and I decided to stay with West Clinic. Dr. Tauer, a Christian man, is Jay's doctor. Jay has malignant melanoma that has not seen a remission point. His first occurrence was in 1995, so our history with this doctor runs deep. Dr. Tauer was also Jay's brother's doctor. Barry died of Hodgkin's disease at age 22 in 1996. Dr. Tauer knows the family history and has already begun genetic testing since pancreatic cancer and melanoma can be genetic.

We have contacted MD Anderson several times and have talked with the head of the GI department, Dr. Abbruzzese. He told us, because of his age, Trey would not be eligible for many of the trials. This is the case with many trials at many institutions. We are VERY BLESSED an adult cancer center is treating Trey.

There are two kinds of pancreatic cancer. Cancer which can form in the ducts called adenocarcinoma (Trey's kind) and endocrine. Trey's, the most common, is very aggressive. When leaving West Clinic, we found out the biopsies of his pancreas from the ERCP at Methodist came back positive. That didn't surprise me.

We made it home from West Clinic and Trey was WORN OUT! He left out the back door throwing up, so we know something different will need to be done for the next treatment. At home, he cannot have any medications by IV except for his pain pump and the TPN, his nutrients. He does not like the TPN. It is in bags that look like IV solution and must be kept refrigerated. Before the TPN can be administered, we have to take it out of the refrigerator and make sure it is warm. He carries this on a pole or in a back pack.

At home, we received assistance from Methodist Hospice/Home Health. We are not in ANY WAY calling it HOSPICE! One nurse came to make sure we could hook up his TPN correctly. Another is the home health nurse. The laws for children are different. When a child is ill, home health care is more accessible. When the nurse asked us about end of life decisions, I reminded her that this was home health care and we would take care of those decisions when that day comes. A nurse will come three times a week (of course, they won't be as pretty as the nurses at St. Jude!) and they are available to us 24/7. Do you see how God is taking care of us through nursing, doctors, and procedures?

It came time for Trey to take his medications and he was not able to hold down anything! Everything came back up, several times! I got in touch with his St. Jude doctor. She told me to give the medications a second time, a few at a time, in 15-30 minute intervals. I only gave the medications I knew he absolutely needed. Medications COVERED the cabinet in his room. I was so nervous giving second doses of medications I had just given him 15 minutes prior, but Dr. Sara assured me the medications were not in his system long enough to take effect. I sat and watched him for 30 minutes. Thankfully he kept those down and slept. All the while he was saying, "Mom, I got this."

He woke up this morning wanting to eat. I said you bet! He took nausea medications first and held down applesauce. This is the first real food he has eaten in ten days. Actually, I'm losing count of how long it's been. Later, he wanted crackers and kept that down. He managed to sit on the couch and watch the U of M basketball game with our new black lab puppy, Abbie. As I gazed in the room at one point, I saw Julianne leaned toward one end of the couch and Trey leaned toward the other with Abbie snuggled between them, covered in blankets. Neither of them looked comfortable, but I was not going to wake them. I thought it might give me time to sit, if for just a moment.

Friends from church and school have come by to visit all day. It was so good to hear him laughing with his friends from school, taking selfies, and laughing at his dad for getting his truck stuck in the backyard. I could see the look on Trey's face. I knew he wanted to get off the couch to help, but he didn't have the strength. Thank goodness for strong football friends that can push a truck!

My sisters came over with the rest of the family. It was a shock for them to see Trey carry his pole down the stairs with all his medications. My sister, Judy, and my niece, Becky, brought Trey a card.

Before he read it, he asked, "It's not a get well card, is it?"

I'm not so sure they got his humor!

I sat for an hour and didn't make it nearly a fourth of the way through the stack of cards and letters we have received. What a blessing! I hope Trey and I can go through a lot of them together tomorrow. His strength comes and goes, but he really wants to look through each card and letter. Donna came over to help me sort through cards, bills while trying to figure out what to keep and what to throw away. Trey was so proud to tell them he had not pushed his pain button since yesterday. We don't think he realizes he is getting an hourly dose of Dilaudid through his IV. Trey was able to eat Kentucky Fried Chicken and mashed potatoes. About 6:30 p.m. he finally said he didn't feel good and I asked family to say goodbye for the evening so we could get him in bed. Now he is resting and eating a pudding snack pack as I pray - please stay down!

At one point, when Trey and I were reading the international cards, we had to translate them over the internet. We had a good time going through the stack of cards trying to read them in different languages.

A friend, Ricky Brethrick, has set up another way to honor Trey throughout the year. Check out www.tailgate4thecure.org. As much as Trey loves football and loves University of Tennessee football, we believe this is a great way to work together to help Trey and help get the name of Tailgate for the Cure out there. Look for Tailgate for the Cure at Collierville on the Square with #prayfortrey products.

Would you believe I have not used the Internet or Google once to research pancreatic cancer? I think it would do more harm than good. There is so much information that I would probably not understand and I truly believe Satan can use confusion to undermine our faith. There is so much knowledge at the tip of my fingers in St. Jude and

West Clinic. Scripture tells me, *"Be anxious for nothing..."* Phillipians 4:6-7. Also, on my desk at home, I'm reminded of the power of prayer:

> *"Pray for anything and if you have faith, you will receive it." Matthew 21:22*

March 12, 2012

I knew the time would come when Trey was stable enough for me to go into work. Just as I get settled at work, Jay calls me from West Clinic. Trey has fever of 100.7. That's not much, right? Anything over 100.4 can be devastating for a cancer patient. Apparently, it is from an underlying infection. They don't know where it started but are checking to see if it's a bladder infection. A bladder infection? You are kidding? How in the world could Trey have a bladder infection? I have to just stop asking questions and get to Trey. Fact is fact. There is an infection.

They are going to try to keep him from going back into the hospital by giving him IV antibiotics daily at West Clinic. Jay told West Clinic the last IV antibiotics Trey received at St. Jude made him itch all over. Those nights were miserable for him. Hopefully they will take care of this with IV Benadryl.

Chemotherapy is going on today, as scheduled. In true Trey fashion, he tweets *"First day of treatment"* and attaches a picture of his IV pole with medications for Instagram. He cannot eat or touch anything cold for four days - no cold Sprite, water, meats, etc. This will get worse over the course of a couple of days during the chemotherapy and, then, subside. It has nothing to do with his cancer, just his chemotherapy treatment.

We are praying this infection clears up and he tolerates the chemotherapy and side effects - diarrhea and mouth sores. And pray for his mama who is at work with nausea because she wants to be with her baby. I just can't concentrate.

Fox News came out to interview Trey today. I was so impressed with how much they cared about Trey. It seemed that he was not just another story. We made new friends with a Fox News reporter and I feel I can trust them. Trey's tweet was *"Just interviewed by fox 13 news everyone check it out airs at 9 tonight!"* Hopefully, they will air what he said about his faith and not the fact it was his first day of treatment. His third Instagram picture of the day was his chemo bags hanging on their poles. How comforting! I think for Trey was just saying, "Okay, let's go!"

> **Julianne Shiles' Thoughts:** Late one night we had been talking about this and that. He kissed me and said, "I think I've found the cure for cancer. Whenever you are here, I don't feel sick at all."

CHAPTER 7

HOW GOD COMES TOGETHER

"There are only two ways to live your life. One is as though nothing is a miracle. The other is as though everything is a miracle." - Albert Einstein

March 14, 2012

I know I don't need to apologize for saying this, but it has just been a crazy week. I have gone back to work and Jay is the main caregiver during the day. Bless his heart. Who better to take care of our son than a paramedic, right? My precious husband, how I love him. ANOTHER one of God's great plans.

Over 20 years ago, Jay's father fell out of a tree and Jay came on the scene. Jay didn't know what to do. At that time, he decided to become a paramedic and never have the helpless feeling again. Of course, we know that God already knew Jay's purpose would be multifaceted. He would have the perfect training to take care of our son. Before we left St. Jude, we had to be trained on how to handle certain equipment and how to take care of Trey's lines. Thank the Lord I didn't even need to listen! God has a place and a plan for each of us. Jay has not left Trey's side. One thing we didn't think about when we came home on March 9, just five days ago, was Trey's room is upstairs and our room is downstairs. Trey has a comfortable recliner in his room that belonged to his Papaw. Jay has been sleeping in this recliner until we feel he can get better adjusted. We also bought a baby monitor with a two-way speaker. We'll see how long it lasts.

We didn't know what was making Trey so sick, the the chemotherapy or the antibiotics. He was throwing up as late as last night. Have I said how much I love St. Jude? I LOVE ST. JUDE! NOT to take anything away from West Clinic. Yesterday I made a couple of trips to St. Jude and found my precious friend, Karen Williams. I poured my heart to her about how Trey cannot tolerate pills any longer. She was amazing! She got on the phone and, BAM, had nausea medications ordered for him that are not pills. I never considered how hard it is just to swallow a simple pill, even if it is the size of a pin head.

Trey's trips to West Clinic the last couple of days are taking a toll on him. He's dealing with chemotherapy, antibiotics, steroids, throwing up, coming home to 10 million medications, nurses, nutritionists, reporters and social workers. Occasionally, we approve a visit by mom and dad from friends. Last night, he begged us to skip the Ativan so he could watch the Grizzlies basketball game. He's gotta watch the Grizz!

"Sorry bud," I answered. "TAKE the medications! I'M GOING TO BED!"

We were so blessed by what The Q 107.5 and 101.9 did yesterday. What an incredible job they did of raising awareness of pancreatic cancer. I want to make it clear. Even though the event was called Radio Trey, we are not raising awareness of Trey. We want to raise the awareness of the light of Jesus in his life. Anyone that knows Trey personally already knows this. For those who don't know Trey, I pray the faith and hope he has in his Savior is evident. He'll be the first to say he does not want the attention directed toward himself. When the church was making shirts with #prayfortrey, he asked for one without #prayfortrey on it. He didn't want that put on his back to draw more attention to him. He knows people are praying for him. He knows where his help comes from and he is secure. He also knows he needs the prayers of God's people to sustain him and to gain the miracle needed to beat this nasty disease.

So many people have been so sweet to ask about Collin. He's doing okay. He has his phone, is on spring break and planning his social calendar. I am so thankful for my "posse", a group of women that have stepped in to take care of our house, our dogs, our laundry, our meals, and our Collin. We are keeping a close eye on him. I realized this morning he was a little scared to go upstairs. He's been sleeping on the couch downstairs because it's spring break. When I asked him to go check on Trey, he said, "Mom, please don't make me do that." Then it hit me. I think we are going to plan a movie night in Trey's room this weekend. Trey loves Collin SO much and it would break Trey's heart to know he was scared. Collin's teachers are being so kind to take extra steps to help him as we walk down this path.

Trey, trying to get some normal back in his own life, has been working on his NCAA bracket and tweeted his final four predictions.

I don't know what I would do without my sisters, Judy and Donna, and Cindy Few, Hollee Lott, and Karen Stonebrook. There are so many others that have been behind the scenes, I am sure. There comes a time that you have to let go and let others take care of you. These precious women are allowing us to take care of our child and caring for us at the same time. I have not told Trey, but today I will be calling to make arrangements for homebound school. I think this is what he needs to complete the year of school. It will not be as bad as he thinks. From what I understand from his counselor at Collierville, when he is feeling well, he can still come to

Collierville and sit in on several classes, but will not get credit. This will feed his social and emotional needs. We just don't need for him to get behind. I really don't see him being able to sit though class, but I am willing to let him try.

Trey goes today to remove his chemotherapy pump for his last treatment this week. We hope he will be feeling better this weekend. He woke up with some pain this morning. He has started on some steroids which we hope will reduce some inflammation of the pancreas or liver or whatever might be causing the nausea. Doctors don't seem to think the nausea is because of the chemotherapy. His jaundice has crept back, so his bilirubin is probably up which can cause nausea. The TPN can also cause nausea. HE DID EAT A PIECE OF TOAST last night and kept it down!

One thing I learned before leaving St. Jude was what all of the important levels of his blood work meant. Amylase and lipase enzyme counts are very important. These are the enzymes produced by the pancreas that help digest food. His Lipase was 1,079 when we left the hospital. While we were at St. Jude, this number fluctuated much higher. It should be around the normal of 150-160. His bilirubin, which is the yellow pigment that is in everyone's blood and stool, should be in the normal range of 0.3 to 1.9 mg/dL. Trey's has been as high as 4.8. There are many other counts Jay and I watch, such as his AST and ALT, other enzymes found in his liver that are running high and out of their normal range. We also watch white blood count, eosinophils, and his lymphocytes. If only we could use a thermometer to monitor these counts!

I want to share a couple of God moments. Nothing is a coincidence with God. Remember, just as he says in Jeremiah 29:11, He has a purpose.

"For I know the plans I have for you," declares The Lord, "plans to prosper you and not to harm you, plans to give you hope and a future. Then you will call on me and come and pray to me, and I will listen to you."

The doctor we have now at St. Jude was not supposed to be assigned to us. But, during clinic, she said she would take the case. We have fallen in love with her and she with us. She has blessed us. She checks in with us every day by text or call. I cannot say enough about Dr. Sara Federico.

Also, the Corum nurse, who coordinated his TPN the first night Trey came home from St. Jude, lives in Collierville. Her stepchildren go to Collierville with Trey. And, I grew up with her husband. I'll never forget how sweet she was coming over the night we came home. We were so tired. I was so scared having Trey home with this *thing* hooked up to him and she made us feel like we could call her at any time.

Going further, the nurse who took care of Trey during his procedures at West Clinic lives in Collierville and her children go to school with Trey. Neal Davis, in radiology, is the husband of my best friend at work, Becky Davis. We have been friends for over 20 years. Neal took care of him during both of his procedures at West Clinic and, emotionally, held us up. He held me up, at least. One way I know I can stand to be at work is I know Trey is being cared for by Neal, Jay and the fine staff at West Clinic. Trey always knew he would receive the best care at West Clinic.

Every time we turn around, God puts two particular men, Keith Cochran and Ron Norton, in the room with us or in the path within reach. These two men are so precious to our family. In our book, there are NO finer two men. Our love overflows for them and their families. We believe NONE of this is coincidence. It is all a part of God's great plan for Trey's life. When we look at the blessings God has bestowed on us, how can we NOT feel blessed? How can we not feel strong? We know where our strength is coming from. We know God is there for us every step.

Last night, Jay asked, "How in the world do people make it through things like this without Christ?"
His mother replied, "Honey, I just don't know."

Continue to pray for Trey! We still believe in miracles. We hope that came across in Trey's interview with a television station today. He showed the reporter where his lines were, what medications he was taking, and what they did to him.

"Three weeks ago I had 100 followers on Twitter," he told the reporter. "Today, I have 2,300, because people have been spreading 'Pray for Trey.' It's amazing how things can move so fast." The most important thing he said in the interview showed his true character. "The hardest thing for me to go through," he said, "is telling people to stop crying. It'll be all right. We'll get through this and everything."

At the same time they were interviewing Trey, I was being interviewed on Court Square while at work. It is amazing how the final piece I saw on TV was edited. That is not what I said! I was very proud of Trey but very upset what I had told the reporter was taken out of context. I was asked if we would have medical expenses. My answer was, yes, I am sure we will have medical expenses. I went on to say we have been blessed because all our medical expenses are being covered by St. Jude including all our expenses at West Clinic. That part didn't make it in the interview.

Needless to say, people were upset to hear a St. Jude patient would have medical expenses. I have been a bundle of emotions since it aired. I have been angry, I have been teary, and I have been scared. So, I called Trey's sweet nurse practitioner, Karen Williams. She came to our house and, while she was here, I was blessed to have Richard Shadyac, CEO of ALSAC, call me. He assured me anything we needed would be taken care of by St. Jude and we were to call him if we needed ANYTHING. Now I know how Trey feels to be overwhelmed with the media! I am so thankful St. Jude has our back, not only when it comes to taking care of my child, but when it includes taking care of my family too. St. Jude is a place where miracles happen.

CHAPTER 8

WHAT A DIFFERENCE A DAY MAKES!

"No one will be able to stand against you all the days of your life. As I was with Moses, so I will be with you; I will never leave you nor forsake you." Joshua 1:5

March 16, 2012

I can honestly say, thank goodness it is Friday. Trey is feeling so much better than he was earlier in the week. He is still tired, but has not dealt with throwing up since Wednesday. Well, maybe Tuesday. Honestly, one day starts to run into the other. I try very hard not to pick up the phone every hour to call home and check on him. I am so thankful he is a teen that likes to text his mama!

After he had his chemo pump removed on Wednesday, he felt so much better that afternoon and on Thursday. Today he has been resting, dealing with nausea and trying to watch basketball. Today, he had his pain pump adjusted. The pain block he had a week ago worked so well we are weaning him off the continuous flow of Dilaudid to just a bolus of pain medications. He'll be able to push his pain pump every 15 minutes if needed. So far, he has been handling that well. Eventually, we will go to pain medications by mouth and pray his stomach can handle it.

He is still on steady medications for nausea and a steroid, which is helping his appetite. He has been eating. As much as he wants to eat, we are being careful what we allow him to eat. We don't want to upset the flow.

There is a chance his counts will drop at the beginning of the week. He had blood drawn on Wednesday. As of right now, all of his counts are steady. We didn't receive his bilirubin count, one of the most important counts I watch!

Not sure what the hang up is there. We will be watching and PRAYING for no fever at the beginning of the week. His color is very good.

Jay accomplished a lot yesterday. He was able to get all of his medical supplies in one large cabinet downstairs in our living room. This is close to the stairs so we can access anything we need very easily. Trey cannot have cold drinks or food, so we have put his drinks in this cabinet. If he does accidentally get a hold of a cold drink, it will make him feel like his airway is closing. All we need is a panicking 15 year old!

We had a sweet surprise yesterday! A lot of young men from Collierville Middle School and Collierville High School mulched and cut our yard. It was nice to give and receive some hugs. Thank you James Crocker and Dan Holcomb!

As Trey is more and more in the media, we have been able to watch and grasp exactly how he is handling his diagnosis. We are very proud of him. We wish some of the stations actually aired more of the meat of the story that is important to us. Capitalizing on a 15 year old with terminal cancer gets them the news coverage they desire but uniting a community to pray is more important to us. Those that know our family, know our heart. Our church knows our heart. Believe it or not, our physicians know our hearts.

First and foremost, we want Trey healed. We believe healing comes through prayer. God gave us physicians to administer the talent of medicine. God has given them such wisdom and we pray and ask for guidance for them daily. We ask others to pray for the doctors as they help Trey daily. The nurses, doctors and staff are wonderful people! We love them all. One thing edited out of Trey's last interview was his request for the community to remember and pray for other St. Jude patients just like him.

I often hear "I cannot imagine what you are going through. You are so strong." I wish I could video our 8 hour day. I think the camera man would quit! There is a definition I have read for faith says it's "holding fast to unseen goodness...the true anesthesia of the soul. Fear becomes dead to men of faith, and the knife may cut without hurting."

> *"Is anyone among you sick? Let him call among the elders of the church, and let them pray over him, anointing him with oil in the name of the Lord; and prayer offered in faith shall save the sick, and the Lord shall raise him up, and if he has committed sins, they will be forgiven him." James 5:14-15*

Oh, and Trey says, GO TIGERS!

March 16, 2012

One bad thing about cancer is how quickly it changes. One minute, the patient feels fine and the next minute, it's hard to know what has hit you. Within the last five hours, the chemotherapy effects have hit Trey. He is very nauseated and so extremely tired he cannot stay awake. He slept the entire time the nurse was here this afternoon. Trey tweeted *"Because your love never fails, never gives up, never runs out on me!"* and then the rest ended. Because he slept all afternoon, he was up all night when he tweeted *"Can't sleep now cause I slept all day, #smartchoices ohwell."*

Trey is not only a Memphis Tiger fan, but a Tennessee Vols fan as well. How can that be? Derek Dooley, the head coach of the University of Tennessee Vols football team, called yesterday and left a message on my cell phone. I am never away from my phone! I only wish I could have bottled the smile on Trey's face when he heard the message to him on my phone. PRICELESS! It's the little things . . . Trey tweeted, *"Focus on HIM, and you will receive peace in his presence"*

That smile didn't last and the night seemed to drag minute by minute. I often wonder why things tend to happen at night. I thought Trey was running fever. He was acting very anxious, having tremors, extremely nauseated, but had been sleeping off and on all day until that point. While we were taking his temperature, his doctor sent me a text to check on him. I thought since he had been sleeping all day, he was starting to feel the effects of the chemotherapy and experiencing the extreme tired feeling we were told he would feel. As I talked to the doctor, we realized the change in behavior occurred after the nurse had been out and had removed the basal rate of his pain pump.

By the time Jay returned from Walmart at 9:45 p.m. with a new thermometer, he had no fever and had been crying. This was not something we had experienced with Trey. He went from pacing the floor to punching the wall to crying. We had given him every medication we could think of to calm him. It was not like he was having seizures; it was more like he was cold and couldn't get warm. It is late on a Friday night. Who do I call? It's so hard to keep panic from showing! I was pushing his bolus every 15 minutes to get Dilaudid in his system when we realized he was experiencing withdrawal from the Dilaudid. It was like a light bulb went off for Jay and me. How could we not have known this would happen? It won't happen again! I'm so thankful we had Dr. Sara to walk us through this scary night.

We reached the nurse by 10:45 p.m. and she arrived around 11 p.m. By that time, the Dilaudid was back into his system and he had calmed down. The doctors ordered for the basal rate to be continued along with his bolus. In layman's terms, they took him off his continuous feed of pain medications yesterday and he only had his pump to push to wean him so he could begin to take pain medications by mouth. At the dosages he was taking and for the length of time he had be on the medicine, quitting "cold turkey" was not a good idea. Needless to say, he has everything back he had when he left St. Jude. He didn't get to sleep until 3 a.m. and I didn't sleep well either. He is having some crazy dreams, but we are getting some good laughs.

What would I have done if his doctor had not sent me a text at the right time to check on him? What a life saver! She kept me calm when I had no idea what was going on and Trey was punching the wall.

The next morning, we traded text messages:

TREY: "Are you awake? Or is the baby thing not working?"
LISA: "Yep. It's not working. What's up? Baby thing not working."
TREY: "Um can I have a bowl of captn crunch?"
LISA: (hesitant): "With milk?"
TREY: (with growing knowledge of his medicine) "If I can have the rubbing medicine on the wrist with the clear wrap on it."

He is talking about Phenergan gel with a tegaderm patch over the medication to keep it from coming off so it will soak into his skin. So this is how we communicate. He is upstairs and we are downstairs, so we either call each other on our phones or text. We have the two-way baby monitor hooked up, but, as we suspected, he does not like it. He had his cereal and kept every bite down. He has eaten well today. He acted like a turkey sandwich and a small plate of a chicken casserole was Thanksgiving dinner.

He has had a lot of visitors today. Needless to say he is worn out! While he was out of the bed we changed his sheets. Then, we gave him his medications and have tucked him in for the night. I went to bed thinking about the talk we had this morning about the devotional he read in Jesus Calling, which he reads every morning when he wakes up. He tweeted part of the devotional.

> *Come to Me for understanding, since I know you far better than you know yourself. I comprehend you in all your complexity; no detail of your life is hidden from Me. I view you through eyes of grace, so don't be afraid of My intimate awareness. Allow the light of My healing Presence to shine into the deepest recesses of your being--cleansing, healing, refreshing, and renewing you. Trust Me enough to accept the full forgiveness that I offer you continually. This great gift, which cost Me My Life, is yours for all eternity. Forgiveness is at the very core of My abiding presence. I will never leave you or forsake you.*

> *When no one else seems to understand you, simply draw closer to Me. Rejoice in the One who understands you completely and loves you perfectly. As I fill you with My Love, you become a reservoir of love, overflowing into the lives of other people. Ps. 139:1-4; 2 Cor. 1:21-22; Joshua 1:5*

> *AND*

> *No one will be able to stand against you all the days of your life. As I was with Moses, so I will be*

with you; I will never leave you nor forsake you."
Joshua 1:5

So tonight, he rests. Our great God comes to give him comfort. More than that, He gives a mother comfort that He is with her son.

Tomorrow we will be thinking about our friend and coach of the Collierville High School Lacrosse team, Steven Shipowitz, who will be running the Germantown Half Marathon #1340 for Trey! 13 miles! Go Steve! Thank you so much!

CHAPTER 9

SUNDAY'S A COMIN'

"Commit your works to the LORD And your plans will be established." Proverbs 16:3

March 19, 2012

What a blessed day is Sunday! Trey's first text of the morning was at 7:39 a.m. I know he had been awake for a long time.

TREY: "Sunday School? Yes or no?"

LISA: "I don't think so. Let's just do big church." I knew just walking out of the house would take so much energy.

TREY: "Ok I just really want some dunkin donuts badly."

LISA: "Ok. We'll get some."

TREY: "So when do I need to get ready?" It's 7:30 in the morning. Church starts at 10 a.m. LISA: "Not now!!!"

TREY: "Okay, just say when!!"

Just to walk through the doors of our church sent a warm feeling through me like the Holy Spirit was filling me for the first time. It was the first time for Trey to go to church in almost a month. Most of his friends had not seen him since he had left church on Saturday night of Disciple Now weekend in February. There were as many stares as there were hugs, but Trey didn't mind. His weight loss is very noticeable and his hair has begun to thin. After the first shower where I saw his hair in the tub, I took a picture. I think it bothers him more than he lets other people know. Maybe he has a little bit of Samson in him after all.

I had the opportunity to join my junior Sunday School girls at the altar before church and pray for Trey, our family, and our church. What a precious time that was to have with them. I have missed being with them on

Sundays and Wednesdays. It is times such as this I realize the return on your investment. I have been teaching some of these young ladies since 9th grade and they have grown very special to my heart and to our entire family. It's what doing life together is all about.

It was very hard for me to concentrate during the service. Being the mama bird that I am, I didn't want to get too far from Trey. It was his first outing with his pump. Also, because of all his medication, Trey did have a tendency say and do odd things. It was a little funny during church when Trey's pump got air in the line and he began to beep. He was afraid that would happen. I could not read his lips when he was a couple of rows up trying to tell Jay and me what was happening. Luckily, all it required was for Jay and Trey to leave the sanctuary to take care of it. I am sure it alarmed people to see Trey get up and leave during the sermon, but Trey and Jay were laughing.

Toward the end of the sermon, we texted

LISA: "Pay attention ;) Tired?"

TREY: "I'm setting up the church outline to my phone. It's pretty awesome! Hannah is helping me!"

LISA: "It is!! I know!"

TREY: "I didn't know that. I just got it set up. My back kills from sitting like this."

I had a feeling he would get sore from sitting in the pew. I was amazed he was able to make it as long as he had.

LISA: "You can leave and go lay down or we can leave when he prays."

TREY: "He's almost done. I think I'll be otay."

He was able to make it through the entire service. I didn't want to rush him out of the church, but I saw how tired he was and knew he had plans for the afternoon. Several of his friends arranged to take Trey to a local park for a picnic. Being out in the fresh air could do him some good. At 3 p.m. I did a little text check:

LISA: "You ok?"

TREY: "Si"

That was good enough for me. I know he was having a good time. We warned him about the heat and told him not to do anything but sit.

Madison Young's Thoughts: Trey was my close friend. From middle school on, we had a bond of Tennessee football and helping each other through some awkward middle and high school relationships. I loved to steal his Phiten necklace every chance I got and he always had to tickle my side so that I would spaz and embarrass myself.

Trey's journey was difficult and sad, but he made the most of every situation, I mean EVERY situation. The first week Trey was in the hospital, his friends were there every chance we got. We were so nervous about what was going to happen that we forgot to eat, so Mr. Jay sent us all downstairs to the café. Trey came along and was waiting for us outside. I walked out first with my food and he started saying he did not feel well and felt like he was going pass out. I went into PANIC mode and started looking for a nurse. He stopped me immediately laughing saying, "Wow you're gullible. Let's trick everyone else!" I was not going to be the dumb blonde who got tricked, so I played along. Trey did the same thing to Cody and Julianne, except they froze and then started backing away. I will forever give them the hardest time about it. Now you see what I mean with making the most of EVERY situation.

Trey was extremely selfless. He was always offering to get me food or a drink and willingly shared his 5lb bag of sour patch kids and skittles with me every time I came over. I owe him big time for introducing me to Riddle Skittles, which happen to be my favorite Skittles in the world. He gave me a handful of Chick fil a coupons, so you can only imagine where we would go to eat! One of my fondest memories about Trey's caring spirit is when I was sitting in his room coloring a Spiderman sheet and we started talking about my prom situation. I got ditched by my date and already had a dress, so I didn't know what to do. Trey being Trey said, "If I had enough energy, I'd go with you, but you should go with...!" and started naming off everyone he could think of. He was sweet and always tried to solve everyone's problems. Our favorite conversation topic was the drama in our lives. We definitely sounded like middle school girls.

He was home by 3:30 p.m. for a visit from a friend, Yancey Gray. Trey didn't know why Yancey was coming by the house to present him with a University of Tennessee football signed by 2012 quarterback Tyler Bray. Trey's face lit up! Jay and I did a good job keeping our mouths shut and not spilling that surprise. Trey said he was so proud of us! He knows his mama can NOT keep a secret from him.

I am amazed Trey was able to rest the afternoon, but his body was beginning to take over. It was very important that he nap before we attempt the Sunday evening service. The Sunday evening service was very special. We had a prayer service for healing in the Faith Building. Stations were set up for different people all over the room that needed different types of healing. Not all healing needed was physical. I cannot explain the overflow of love for Trey. The prayers lifted up for meant so much to us. We know God heard each prayer. It was a very private time for Trey and our church. At the same time, there were people praying over Trey that I had never met. I could never have imagined they would say the words that came out of their mouths on his behalf. Prayer is such a powerful tool. There were hands all over Trey and youth at his feet in tears. This is one time Trey did cry and I am glad it was with his friends. It's a time we will always cherish.

I watched Collin out of the corner of my eye. It was very hard to concentrate my full energy on Trey knowing Collin would be thrown in the middle of this sea of emotions he didn't understand. I am thankful my sister, Donna, had Collin most of the time and kept him occupied. Ron Norton led Under Authority (Germantown Baptist Youth Choir) in a Desert Song by Hillsong that speaks to the presence of God during this time. Trey has sung this song MANY times. It's one of our favorites. To be able to pray, praise, cry and leave feeling fully blessed by our church is something we don't take for granted.

We ask you continue to pray for Trey! We still believe in miracles.

Needless to say, Trey was worn out afterwards. Even when exhausted, he has trouble sleeping. We have added

Ambien to his list of medications to help his insomnia. He didn't seem to sleep any better with the Ambien last night. He is up and down all night going to the bathroom and I worry when I hear him. He has to push his pole with his TPN bag and his pump down the hall to the bathroom across the carpet. I know it takes all the strength he has to make it. What scares me the most is his crossing the opening of the top of the stairs to get to the bathroom. I'm afraid he will fall. Jay has moved downstairs since Trey has not been sleeping. Trey keeps the television on all night long and watches movies over and over. He's been very good about calling when he needs us, but we think the TPN (nutrients) might have something to do with his sleepless nights. And ours too!

We met with his homebound teacher today. As God would have it, she was a teacher Collin had for part of his last school year. She asked, knowing we are Christians, if we were okay talking about our faith. WOW! Who cares if school gets done? I guess Shelby County cares. So God has placed a homebound teacher in our home that believes in our Lord, will teach our son, taught Collin in elementary school, and was part of an IEP meeting for him last year. Trey felt much better after they talked, knowing there would not be pressure on him to get things done like he thought. I loved Trey's tweet today... *"Makes me sad to see everyone complaining about going to school #enjoyit #neverknowwhenyouwontbeabletoo"* I am proud he is standing up to their complaining, but not to draw attention to himself. He also tweeted today from Isaiah 12:2

> *"I will trust in him and not fear, For the LORD give me strength and protects me; he has become my deliverer."*

I cannot begin to explain all the ways God is blessing us, The Caringbridge site is such a blessing for me to read. I receive so many encouraging emails and I am personally overwhelmed. Some days I should not look at my email because they are a little much. If I don't return your email, please know I have read it. I just have not had a chance to respond. Usually, ten things are going on at the same time and I'm reading them from my phone, talking to a nurse, a doctor, my boss, Jay, Trey, Collin, cleaning up after the dogs, fixing food, figuring out which stack the bill goes in (important, not so important, or who cares), answering the door, giving medicines, texting, or who knows. Our door is constantly revolving. And yes, we are tired. But what choice is there? Life goes on with lots of prayer.

There will come a time when we'll have to put a "No Visitors" sign on the door. We hope Trey's friends understand. The adults will have no problem. I think Trey is the one that will have the problem. We tried the sign at St. Jude and he would have no part of it.

I got a call from Coach O'Neill with an idea. He said, since the football team had to run, why not have them run to our house and back to the field? It is about the same distance they normally run. There was a catch. Trey had to get out of bed, walk downstairs and come outside.

Trey now has his days and nights mixed up. It's like we are taking care of a baby. When I told him about the offer, he was in such a state of exhaustion, he asked to just wave from the window. I told him no! Today, with our help, Trey walked almost to the end of the stairway and waved at his teammates. There were boys running from a block away. When they arrived, they lined the yard leaning over, heaving from running and with sweat pouring. I wanted Trey to see them; I wanted them to see Trey. As a mother, I wanted them to appreciate the fact that they were able to run down the street while Trey struggled to climb the stairs, carrying a pole and a bag. I know Trey didn't feel that way. Trey would have given anything to be out there with them. Maybe it was a little cruel to make him walk down the stairs to see them. At this point, though, we needed something for motivation because what we were doing was not working. After the visit, Trey tweeted, *"Thanks to all who came and visited me today no matter how you got here haha but thanks it changed my day around! #loveyall #blessed"* He does love his teammates with all his heart.

We do appreciate everyone who has sent information for different institutions, protocols, clinical trials, etc. Here me when I say, we are so blessed to be allowed the opportunity to be treated at St. Jude and West Clinic. One day, we will be the family with a story for someone else that says go to St. Jude and West Clinic! We are so mindful of God's hand in our journey and we might never have seen that without living it side by side with these doctors in these places. I truly don't understand why physicians are not knocking down our door begging Trey to join their clinical trials, but they are not. Most of the trials require a patient to be 18 years old. In choosing St. Jude and West Clinic, we also weighed the risks of being away from home. For Trey to be able to fight this aggressive cancer, it is more important for him to be at home, surrounded by family and friends who can give him constant love and encouragement.

One reason I'm not reading my email is because we've been receiving email and phone calls that have not been encouraging. One email subject line read: I AM APPALLED. I opened the email, read it, and deleted it. We also receive phone calls asking why we are not choosing various treatments. I'm amazed how heated people can become when I politely refuse. I believe they have taken Trey as their son too. Trust me, I know God is in control.

I know people are praying and I cannot ask for anything thing more. Today, I called a place of business. When I identified myself, the employee responded "OH you are Trey's mama! We are praying for that baby boy!" What a blessing.

We have been blessed become affiliated with Ricky Bretherick and Tailgate for the Cure. They are doing so much for our family. They are raising awareness of Trey's pancreatic cancer and raising funds. During football season, funds will be raised in Trey's honor for St. Jude. Ricky has many things in store for Trey and we are looking forward to being a part of Tailgate for the Cure.

As I think of the different pieces the Erwin family is trying to put together in this crazy puzzle called life, I am reminded of a scripture calling us to be at peace with each other as we each walk different paths.

"Let the peace of Christ rule in your hearts, since as members of one body you were called to peace. And be thankful." Colossians 3:15

March 21, 2012

Home health is actually a blessing. In the beginning, I fought it in my mind, but we would not have been able to survive without having Trey's nurse available to us 24/7. The home health nurse came to check on Trey and took blood to check his counts. Trey didn't have a good night. He threw up most of the night. She took Trey's blood directly to St. Jude and we waited all day to hear from the doctors about his counts. The counts from after the first round of chemotherapy are a good basis for what his counts will be after each round. We have watched the clock all day. ...hurry up and wait.

We have made a little progress with Trey's energy and eating. Trey made a special request for a Chick-fil-A chocolate milkshake around 6 p.m. Unfortunately, his intestines reminded him about it later. Trey has been like a pregnant woman with his Chick-fil-A milkshakes. He cannot seem to get enough. It must be his body craving what the milkshake gives him. It sure gives it right back!

Trey and I were able to curl up in his bed, look at the computer and dream about Hawaii. He has chosen Hawaii for his Make a Wish trip. Who knew there was a Disney resort in Hawaii? His counts being good for the trip is one thing that concerns everyone. We can only hope and pray his body starts to accept the chemotherapy and his counts will be where they need to be when it's time to go. We are grateful to be granted a wish! In some ways, I thought being granted a wish was a sad thing. Later, I learned wishes are granted to some non-terminal patients.

The day was not all bad. Jay and I both received a call from Coach David Cutcliffe. He took the time to talk to Trey and his genuine interest in our family was overwhelming. I think our University of Tennessee pride went straight through the telephone! He said he had contacted a few people and we should be receiving some phone calls. He mentioned having Peyton Manning call, but I don't want Trey do get his hopes up. I think we would have to revive him.

We know something revisited him later in the evening because he could not stay out of the bathroom. Finally, at 2:30 a.m., he was able to go to sleep and Jay and I tried to settle down. I found out this morning Jay didn't sleep either. Too bad neither of us knew. We could have, at least, played Words with Friends with each other. Does bilirubin have two ll's or one?

Trey's tweet this morning was *"The Lord is the Spirit, and where [the] Lord is present there is freedom."* *2 Corinthians 3:17 Have faith in the Spirit and you will be #free!"* This morning, Trey said he didn't sleep well, but that didn't stop him from going to school for the first time since February. He had to get his books, workbooks, etc. to start school at home. From what he told me, everyone was so glad to see him. I know walking those familiar halls did him more good than anyone. He had to love being able to go to his locker, remember his combination and get his books out, like he would on a normal day. We are hoping he will be able to sit in a classroom before the end of the year, just to sit.

Dr. Sara called and his counts are GREAT! WHAT A BLESSING! This is a true answer to prayer. She also told us many people with an ANC count of 6,900 believe the chemotherapy is not working. There is a percentage, however, of people whose counts are close to normal after their first chemo round. I'll take that! We would like to hope the chemotherapy is working without destroying all of his good cells! God can do that! If God, in his infinite wisdom, can form a baby in a mother's womb cell by cell, what makes us think He cannot divide the good cells from the bad cells?

She also told us they have decided to do a scan, hopefully PET, before his third round of chemotherapy. That will be the first week of April. START PRAYING! We are all waiting for God to show Himself in a mighty way. But, I think we all know He is already doing that.

Have you seen a t-shirt lately? Or a yard sign, car decal, or bracelet? Oh, I bet you have. It's hard to commit to pray, isn't it? Please don't take praying lightly. Praying is intimate conversation with God. I was convicted of this today myself. I went to see Keith, who had surgery today. I mentioned how busy Jay and I have been and how it's so hard to stop, slow down, and acknowledge the awesomeness of our God. Sound familiar?

The highlight of the day came during Trey's school hour! His phone rang and it showed BLOCKED. Jay told him not to answer it because he was "at school." Well, it was Eli Manning calling! Eli left a nice message, the SECOND message we have missed from someone "important." Eli kept his word and called back! Trey said he was such a nice guy! They talked about juggling classes and football and he said he would keep in touch. Trey immediately tweeted, *"Just got off the phone with ELI MANNING!!!!! #amazingguy #superblessed #thanks4thesupport"*

Trey was having a great day. Morgan Cox of the Baltimore Ravens visited, brought one of his jerseys and signed it for him. Morgan was so nice just to sit in Trey's room and visit with Trey and his friends. Many photos were taken, of course. Trey also received a package today from the Tennessee Titans organization with a hat, mini helmet, t-shirt and an autographed picture of Jake Locker, quarterback of the Titans.

Tonight, he tweeted, *"MAJOR S/O to ALL my followers even though it's a tough journey. I would be NOWHERE without the support of everyone! I love you all!! #GODBLESS"* At this point, Trey has over 10,000 followers on Twitter. I think it is funny! Recently, D. J. tweeted *"That's crazy... My little guy @treyerwin13 got more followers than me. Ha ha."* We know that will not last long with D. J.'s University of Memphis basketball career.

He has had one full day. Tomorrow will be even busier. Trey asked, seriously, that he not receive any visitors tomorrow. I am very proud of him. He said he needs to rest and just wants to watch television. We will be at St. Jude for most of the morning. We know "most of the morning" could mean all day.

We are eating well and we thank you. The meals Cindy Molnar set up through Take Them a Meal have been a life saver for our family. Trey needs the protein and calories! We have got get him back on the field! There are days we just look in the pantry or refrigerator and our minds are so numb, we cannot even comprehend how to heat up a meal, much less decide what to fix. I don't realize how occupied my mind is until it's time to do simple, daily tasks. These meals allow us to concentrate, 100 percent, on taking care of our family.

Trey's last tweet of the evening was, *"And we know that all things work together for good for those who love God, who are called according to his purpose. Romans 8:28 #AMEN"*

CHAPTER 10

FIRST OUTPATIENT VISIT AT ST. JUDE

"Yet, LORD my God, give attention to your servant's prayer and his plea for mercy. Hear the cry and the prayer your servant is praying in your presence." 2 Chronicles 6:19

March 23, 2012

Trey tweeted early, *"Just arrived at St Jude for more scans and stuff #gonnabealongday"*

Today is our first outpatient trip to St. Jude. We were scheduled in x-ray at 9 a.m. and Clinic D at 10 a.m. to meet with the head of Quality of Life and the doctor. That didn't sound very good to me. Thank goodness for modern technology! I texted the nurse practitioner at St. Jude and she assured us it was nothing to be worried about.

Trey had his x-ray and we saw Dr. Sara (plus Dr. Pappo stuck his head in for usual hugs and kisses!) in Clinic D. Trey has not had a solid "dump", as he calls it, since St. Jude, or before. He's been in pain the last couple of days and the pain he has been describing is different from his pancreas pain. He has been on constant pain medications so we know he could be constipated. The doctors are very concerned about him becoming compacted.

But just like when the television repairman comes and the television decides to work, Trey got to St. Jude and produced a stool sample. That was good! The infectious test was negative! What a blessing! We just have to get his gut to begin working properly. I wish I could post a video of Dr. Sara explaining how it works. She is so precious in her explanations! I love how she draws pictures for us, so simple. I am so glad because I sure need that right now!

We are so overloaded with information. Have I said how much I love St. Jude?

After Trey saw the doctor, they took his vital signs and weighed him. He has now lost 20 pounds. He got very upset, cried, and became very depressed. Seeing everything he had been working toward just wasting away was too much. Jay tried to explain to him it will take a while to get the weight back on, but we will do it!

We really appreciate everyone respecting our wishes for no visitors. Trey was able to take a two hour nap and felt well enough to go watch his church basketball team play. True to form, he came home complaining about how they played. When I asked who was there and not there, he said, "well, Caleb has a broken wrist, so-in-so had soccer, so-in-so had to work, and *I* have cancer."

BAM! Reality hit. Hearing him say it without batting an eye took me by surprise. At the same time, there was a television show on. Collin leaned over and whispered, "Mom, change the channel, hurry, change the channel, they are talking about pancreatic cancer."

How precious. Trey thinks he does not understand. He knows more than everyone thinks he does.

We hope to have a relaxing weekend before he goes for his next chemo on Monday. He's totally off the TPN (nutrients) and eating well. I think he has had a milkshake every day! He still has his pain pump, which he will keep until the abdomen pain is under control. He's been pushing his button quite often. Hence his tweet today, *"On these medications and I'm feeling kinda better but they keep knocking me out"*

Sonya Luna, you are one crazy t-shirt lady! You are everywhere with Trey's shirts. Not to be outdone by the Memphis Fire Department. You might say you are brothers, but you have got sisters too! I wish you could see a picture a friend sent from Arlington High School yesterday!

I mentioned the property values are going to go up in Collierville because everyone is going to want to live in such a wonderful community! We are so blessed.

I want to share something from yesterday and today's <u>Jesus Calling</u>:

> *I do my greatest works through people with grateful, trusting hearts. Rather than planning and evaluating, practice trusting and thanking Me continually. This is a paradigm shift that will revolutionize your life."*

> *I am a God of both intricate detail and overflowing abundance. When you entrust the details of your life to Me, you are surprised by how thoroughly I answer you petitions. I take pleasure in hearing your prayers, so feel free to bring Me all your requests...Come to Me with open hands and heart, ready to receive all I have for you.*

The t-shirt sales, signs, bracelets, etc. is not like a presidential campaign. It has many facets: praying for Trey, connecting with God, bringing awareness to pancreatic cancer and uniting people. Yes, we are praying Trey wins this race. We will never give up praying for healing for Trey here on earth. We know how much we are blessed and all we can do in return is point you to the giver of our blessings!

We ask that you continue to pray for Trey as he tries to rest this weekend. Jay needs rest. I have an upper respiratory infection and our house is a wreck, which is bugging me to death. When it rains, it pours! We had a toilet run all night in our master bathroom and had to rip up all the carpet. Two months ago, we would not have laughed at that! Today, we just said "oh well." Not to mention, I would have never let people in my house looking the way it is. Today, it just does not matter.

Today is Jay's birthday. We asked him what he wanted. He answered, "I want my son well." God hear his plea.

"Yet, LORD my God, give attention to your servant's prayer and his plea for mercy. Hear the cry and the prayer that your servant is praying in your presence." 2 Chronicles 6:19

Trey tweeted, *"Major S/O to @jwe2405 for being the best dad a son could ever ask for! Happy birthday dad love you so much for helping me through everything"*

March 26, 2012

We have had some laughs over the last couple of days and it's been nice. It feels sort of like experiencing a little bit of life before cancer with laughter and sports. We are at the end of a chemotherapy treatment so Trey feels better.

Jay told on me. I didn't know Trey was reading his own carepage. So, Jay ratted me out and said I mentioned his poop! Thanks Jay! He tried to explain to Trey that people want to know how he is doing and, unfortunately, that's all a part of this ugly process. I was sitting downstairs and heard, "MOM!" and I knew. If he only knew some of the things he says when he is on all his medications!

I cannot believe I did it again. I left my phone unattended. And who should call but Peyton Manning? He called back and talked to Trey. The good thing about missing the call is I have a voicemail! Watching Trey talk to his childhood idol on the phone and look at the posters of Peyton on the wall at the same time was a thrill for Jay and me. I cannot say enough good things about the Manning family. It was funny when I told Peyton that Eli had already called. I felt like I was in a commercial. And just like when Eli called, Peyton was just as concerned about Trey's condition and what was in store for his future. Trey tweeted *"I know ya'll prob won't believe me but I just got off the phone with Peyton Manning!!!! #totalsurprise #manningfamilylove #unbelievable"*

The wonder sparkle in his eyes brought back memories of taking him to hear Archie Manning speak at Christ United Methodist Church some years ago. We had a front row seat. Trey was young and hung on Archie Manning's every word. My, how things change in just a short time.

After he got off the phone, the realization of what had just happened sank in. He realized why Peyton was reaching out to him. I walked into his room and Trey was crying.

"Trey, what is wrong! You just got off the phone with Peyton Manning!" I said.

"I know," he said," but I know why he's calling and I just want to be normal. I just want to be normal."

Trey was leaning over the edge of his bed with his head in his hands, tears running down his face and there was nothing I could do. Until now, Trey has not really cried. It takes Peyton Manning to bring him to the point of realizing he is no longer normal.

I immediately called our nurse practitioner to see what could be done. Trey is the one who gives back and serves. Now, he's the one on the other side receiving benefits of mission work and that's hard. We attempted to devise a plan where Trey could give back to the St. Jude community. That way, if someone "important" called, Trey would be able to "pass it on" by asking the person to call them for encouragement. Ultimately, this plan didn't come to fruition because of HIPAA. I didn't explain all of the in's and out's to Trey and why it didn't work out. I just left it open ended and began to pray that God would begin to use Trey in order to encourage him knowing God is our strength and refuge.

The thrush in his mouth bothered him all weekend. So, he went on a binge of having milkshakes two or three times a day and ice cream at around 2 a.m. That is perfectly okay! It's calories coating his tongue and throat. It amazed me he was not able to eat BBQ but can eat something else and, later, eat half a bag of skittles. I cannot even eat skittles on a good day!

Jay and I sleep with our cell phones at our ears. At 1:06 a.m., I receive a text.

TREY: "Are you awake?"

LISA: "Yep"

TREY: "I can't sleep cause I'm so hungry I'm having cramps cause it's empty."

LISA: "What do you want to eat?"

TREY: "Grandma said she brought ice cream...only cause my tongue can't handle anything else. It burns."

LISA: "You want a big bowl?"

TREY: (obviously in his right mind) "Just enough to fill my stomach and sooth my tongue." LISA: "Comin up!"

TREY: "Thank you very much!"

After a couple of hours of sleep it was 8:34 a.m. and I text him.

LISA: "You up? Hungry?"

TREY: "Siiiii"

He went on to tell me his mouth hurt 30 times worse then it had the day before. No matter how much he used the "magic" mouthwash, it didn't help. The mouthwash was proving not to be so magic.

We have adjustments to be made. Collin needs to adjust to the normal routine of doing things knowing that Trey will not be at the regular events, like church. We have a lot of work to do there. It may take time to figure out the logistics of how to make sure Collin is where he needs to be, but he needs to know he is a priority.

Trey has his second chemotherapy treatment today. He saw Dr. Tauer and they have scheduled him for a PET scan for April 9, also the date for his third chemotherapy treatment. Dr. Tauer has given him some Creon to help his stomach. He thinks all the nausea he's been experiencing is from the chemotherapy. The scan will tell for sure. It's amazing how these tests can answer so many questions for the doctors and allow them to adjust the course of treatment for a patient. Dr. Tauer knows Trey is battling severe hunger where everything sounds good, but nothing is satisfying. Once he eats, his stomach gets upset and we are back to square one with his hunger. It is gut wrenching pain and it causes him to bend over, grab his knees and rock back and forth. There is no consoling him until his hunger is satisfied.

I hope you had a chance to drive through Collierville this weekend! It was amazing to see everyone out in of support of Trey. The car wash gals did a great job!

We love you guys and could not make it through this without your support! Trey tweeted, *"Can't express the emotions I have for all you people supporting me thank ya'll soo much. I cannot do it without ya'll #soblessed #amazed"*

Praying for a quiet, painless night.

March 27, 2012

Yesterday was Trey's second treatment at West Clinic. Jay and Trey knew it would be a long day. It is hard for an anxious mama to sit at work while they talk to doctors, nurses, and I am not there to ask questions. Thank goodness for iPhone technology! Patch me in!

Dr. Tauer saw Trey before he started his chemotherapy and said he looked good! The entire time Jay and Trey were with Dr. Tauer, I was texting questions. Jay said he finally just showed Dr. Tauer his phone because as I would ask the exact question, Dr. Tauer would immediately answer. Bless Jay, he needs a break! Don't ask him. He will not take it. He IS the most awesome dad, husband, and caregiver.

One of my questions was about Trey's stomach. Dr. Tauer said his stomach pain could be coming from his lack of pancreatic enzymes. He's been put on a drug called Creon to help his body break down fat in the foods we are giving him. He has to take this medication before every meal and snack. This sounds just like the Pancrealipace he has been taking before every meal and snack since we left St. Jude.

My concern with the stomach is the cancer might have spread. We know cancer is in the duodenum, a small area, connected to the pancreas that assists with breakdown of food. Sometime earlier, we were told the pancreatic tumor likely started growing in the duodenum and grew into the head of the pancreas. We won't know about his stomach until he has a scan, currently scheduled for April 9, the day of his third treatment. I wonder every day where and how fast the cancer spreading. As a mother, I'd like them to do a scan every week, but it's not reasonable. It would not change the protocol of treatment.

Luckily, they are not cutting back on any of his nausea medication. They are, however, cutting back on his pain pump. Eventually, we'd love to have him weaned off of it and only taking pain medication by mouth. We need to get him down to as little medications as we can. I think that is the West Clinic way. If it was up to me, I'd give him anything to make sure he feels better. When we first got home from St. Jude and had all of his medications set out in his room, he wanted them moved behind his television so he could not see as much of them. There were so many! Finally, we got them all moved downstairs.

Trey finally started chemotherapy around noon or so. When I contacted Jay to see how he was doing, he told me he was chatting with Coach Pastner. That will start chemotherapy off right! As Trey tweeted during his treatment *"chillin in west clinic, getting second round of chemo...#bring it on"* When I got home, I asked him how he was feeling.

"Like I just got chemo," he answered.

After Trey had finished school for the morning, I sent him a text.

LISA: "Yeah! School is out! Now rest."

TREY: "Nothing like potato soup and the lion king in a comfy bed."

LISA: (at work and jealous) "I would say so!"

TREY: "How is work?"

Oh my. How is work? If he only knew all I could do was think about him 24/7.

After he got a good nap, he ate his bowl of potato soup, two plates of lasagna with bread AND kept it down! That's the good part. Then, he started loading music on a computer. The bad part is he didn't sleep all night because they loaded him with steroids during the chemo. Thank goodness for ESPN and college basketball!

He was quite cranky this morning because he had to do homework before the teacher came. He did make a 100 on a geometry quiz. I think he likes this homebound stuff.

We are hoping he will be able to rest this afternoon. We know the chemotherapy today and tomorrow will catch up to him by the weekend. We hope it won't be as bad as the last treatment. We'll stay on top of the mouth sores and make sure he is getting calories. Even tough the weight loss really bothers Trey, Dr. Tauer said he could lose a little more weight and be okay. He has lost 20 pounds total. Twenty pounds that were hard for him to gain in the first place. He worked all summer drinking protein drinks and working out to put on the weight.

So many people have asked about our precious Collin. He is a silent sufferer. He's not doing well in school and I am so thankful the Collierville Middle teachers are staying after school to help him with this work. They are striving to get him through this year. So many of our church friends have taken him in and been there when we have needed them. We really appreciate it. Trey is not neglecting Collin. They play games together and Collin will sleep in the recliner in Trey's room, until Collin starts snoring and Trey throws things at him. Actually, Trey will throw things at him multiple times. He is his father's son.

God is continuing to bless us as we walk down an unknown path. We know there will be many more days of ups and downs. We are thankful we have a God who already knows what those ups and downs are and is there to prepare the way for us. Trusting in Him, daily, is what we have to do. Yes, there are mornings I wake up and think I cannot get out of bed and do this. Then, one foot hits the floor and I remember my God is sovereign and He'll carry me all day long. I don't have to worry about anything.

There is that peace again..."*When peace, like a river, attendeth my way....*"

March 29, 2012

Trey ate twenty-eight pizza rolls Tuesday night. That is normal for a teenager, but not so normal for someone with a chemotherapy pump, nausea medications, and having trouble getting out of bed. So I am thankful, even if it is pizza rolls!

As far as food is concerned, the doctors have said, if he wants it, give it to him. He will be the one to suffer later, which he did. But he is doing that with all food so it does not really matter what he eats. Why not do it up right! It just drains him, literally, to go back and forth to the bathroom for hours. It is amazing what control a 6 inch long organ has over your body!

It was time for the football team to run again so I sent Trey a text.

LISA: "The football team will be there around 2:40 running from the school. Be prepared to walk to the mailbox and maybe down the sidewalk with them."

TREY: "Can they do it tom?"

LISA: "We'll see. Don't worry about it. Just rest."

Instead, my nephew, Bobby, came over. With encouragement from Bobby, Trey made it around the cove and down our street twice! I am so proud of him. But it wore him out. He needed to research the excursions for his Hawaii trip, so he crashed in the chair and proceeded to search the computer.

We received a test back from St. Jude and his fat content was very high. We knew his pancreas was not able to break down the fat his body was taking in. He went back to West Clinic yesterday to have his pump taken off for this round of chemotherapy. While he was there, Phillip Fulmer, former coach of the University of Tennessee Vols called. He had called me and I told him to call there. Thank you Duke Clement for making that contact for us!

Just a two hour outing to West Clinic takes everything out of him so Tuesday night was very quiet for us and a nice time for Trey and Collin. It was also a nice time for Jay and me to visit with my long time best friend, Dawn Shackelford. I'm not so sure Jay appreciated having to watch Dancing With the Stars but he did it anyway.

Yesterday was the first day I had experienced being "down." I know, I will have many more of those days. I don't know why it hit yesterday. I could list a number of reasons I suspect. I would much rather be home with my son and contributing to his care than working. I guess working is contributing to his care. To my surprise I had a friend, Angie Garrett, show up at work with my favorite chocolate! That will brighten anyone's day! So I got to go home with my OWN candy!

Fox News called yesterday to ask how Trey was doing. The reporter who initially interviewed him was so sweet to ask about him and the events for fundraising that are coming up. I gave her the information and the people she could contact. She let me know that it would be on at 9 p.m. I was so proud to see they talked to one of Trey's friends at Harding Academy. The Harding Academy family is such a blessing. Jay and his brothers went to high school there and we stay in touch with many still involved at the school.

I enjoy my late night talks with Trey. Last night he was so anxious to "do something." He kept saying I got to "do something." He commented people should realize this may be your only chance and not to waste it. He has always been a doer, i.e. mission trips, working in yards, building things, singing in nursing homes, car washes. He said it is so awesome to see how God is touching all these people and how Jesus is speaking to so many people, but he wishes he could be more of a part of it. We are out in the world, seeing things going on around us while all he sees are the four walls of his bedroom. We are praying he has the strength to get up and start moving around today. First thing, he wants donuts this morning and his dad said he had to get up and go with him. He said OK!

He reads his devotional book Jesus Calling every morning and does his quiet time. I called him this morning and told him Sarah Young, the author of Jesus Calling, had signed his guestbook. He said the timing was cool because he had just finished reading this morning's devotion.

Today's verses are very appropriate for what he is feeling in his frustration of wanting to help and see what God is doing in this world.

> "I have told you these things, so that in me you may have peace. In this world you will have trouble. But take heart! I have overcome the world." John 16:33

> "There is a time for everything, and a season for every activity under heaven." Ecclesicates 3:1

Jesus Calling says,

> Accept the limitations of living one day at a time. When something comes to your attention, ask Me whether or not it is part of today's agenda. If it isn't, release it into My care and go on about today's duties.

We should all learn from that. Not just Trey. We are praying Trey gains strength each day! But most of all, the DESIRE to gain strength.

Bobby Thorne's Thoughts: I can remember walking into Trey's room to hang out one afternoon. Taylor Johnson was already there. They were preparing to play NBA 2K when Trey asked me to play for him since he didn't feel well. He reassured me it would be hilarious to watch me play against Taylor since I had never played the game before. As a joke, I found the worst team in the game – the Charlotte Bobcats - just to make sure it was really comedic. Taylor had chosen the Clippers. Needless to say I was in trouble. We played through all four quarters and I had no idea what I was doing. Taylor was only winning by a point as I managed to obtain the last possession. I can still remember the breakaway between Kemba Walker and Blake Griffin. To this day, I have no idea how I did it, but I somehow euro stepped around Blake and laid it in right at the buzzer. Trey was laughing so hard, he couldn't believe I'd just won with the worst team in the game. I told him I won it for him! It was a great time for us to just mess around and laugh. Taylor asked for a rematch and to this day we still haven't played against each other.

CHAPTER 11

A NEW PERSPECTIVE

"I will praise you forever, O God, for what you have done. I will trust in your good name in the presence of your faithful people."
Psalms 52:9

March 31, 2012

Thursday ended up not being a good day after chemotherapy ended for the three day period. Trey's teacher was only able to stay 30 minutes before he had to go to bed. I think trying to put an hour and a half of school in just after chemotherapy is a little much when he has not even been able to get out of the bed for any period of time. Next week, school will only be for one hour a day. I think he will be able to handle that much better. There are nights he is up at 11 p.m. trying to do homework for the next day. Frustration overcomes his body and anger turns to tears. At that point, I just tell him to stop. It is not worth it. I told his teacher about it the next day and she said they could work on homework together and to never let him get to that point. That was such a blessing for Trey, but he still obsessed about getting his work done.

Even though he was not feeling well, he had his favorite meal of poppyseed chicken on Thursday and good friends, Taylor and Anna Wakefield, came to visit. It was good to hear him laugh a little. Those are moments I remember and smiles I capture in my mind. I'll always remember Taylor in the floor, Anna in the chair, Trey in the bed, and everyone talking basketball. All Trey has been doing is watching basketball on television.

Trey was looking forward to not having to get up for anything on Friday morning ~ no doctors, nurses, tests, school, etc. So, Jay and Trey decided to visit IHOP. He needed to get out. I don't think things taste as good in reality as they do in his mind. The chemotherapy taste has set in.

He did see the home health nurse on Friday when they reduced his pain pump. He is not having pancreatic pain, so we need to wean him from the pump gradually, but quickly. He is doing well with that. He still needs to push his button some. Today, though, he had a headache and, instead of pushing the button for immediate relief, he took Advil. He is using the pump for the stomach cramps.

On Friday, I hit my wall at work. After his bad day on Thursday and knowing I could not be home to help, comfort, or just be in the house, I knew it was time to say I cannot do this anymore. I work for wonderful people who are willing to be very flexible in this situation. I worked as long as I could with the unknown future. Actually, I think we all work that way. I know God will take care of our family.

Trey still was not very active on Friday. Jay promised to take him and Collin to Baskin Robbins but it still took a lot of prompting to get him out of the bed and out of the house. Renee Teate and I were sitting downstairs when he came downstairs and said "Let's do this." And off they went. He wanted to make sure Ms. Renee was here when he got back.

The cold effect from his chemotherapy has worsened and has carried over a little longer than four days so he wasn't able to eat the shake he got. We accepted that as he got further into the treatments. He has had trouble drinking cold drinks during the day which is very frustrating. Who likes to drink warm water with a hand full of pills? As the weekend has gone on, he has worked on the shake and been able to slowly eat it.

There was a lot going on today. Trey "stuff" was being sold at the Bartlett Baptist Market, somewhere on Beale Street, and at the lacrosse tournament at Johnson Park. We feel very blessed by all the people who have taken an interest in our family and our son. It is an unconditional love. I think we received the greatest blessing by the knock on our door today from a neighbor whose little girl had a lemonade stand for Trey. We took her upstairs to give the money to Trey. How precious for her to give what she earned to Trey! He was so touched and humbled. It is such an example of the widow in Luke 21:1-4 who gave Jesus all she had, not that Trey is Jesus, by any means.

We talked all day about getting out of bed. Trey knows it's important to get downstairs every day. Jay finally had to get strong with him and tell him how things will start shutting down if he doesn't make the effort to move around. Bobby has been a constant at our house and has filled a lot of empty time for Trey. Bobby, Laura Teate, and Lainey Ortega got Trey out and he walked around the corner. Jay and I were amazed. When he gets something in his mind, he goes and goes. He came back, walked right by our house and kept going. When he got back he smiled and said, "I think I'm going to go sit down."

He ate dinner downstairs, a major accomplishment, and watched the ballgames with us! We are praying this will show him he can do it and feel okay. Maybe, he'll do the same tomorrow. We never know what the next day will bring.

Tomorrow is the Ali Mills 5k at St. George's Episcopal School to benefit Trey. I will go tomorrow afternoon to accept the check. It's quite an honor to be recognized.

We have a little trip we are looking forward to in April. We have been invited to the Orange and White game at the University of Tennessee on April 21. Thank you Coach

Fulmer, Chris Fuller, the Alumni Association, and the anonymous donors for making that happen. We look forward to spending this weekend in Knoxville with Trey as an honorary alumni for a day! He's dreamed of attending UT since he was very young.

Trey's doctor shared a scripture with me this week as we approached Palm Sunday. So many have asked if we have asked ourselves why? As Jesus was suffering during those last days and drops of blood flowed from his head, he did ask God if He was willing to take this cup from Him. Ultimately, Jesus wanted His will to be done. People still ask why Jesus had to be crucified. It was for our sins. The verse Dr. Sara gave to me was John 13:7:

"What I am doing, you do not understand not, but you will understand later."

This is where our faith comes in. We have faith and peace that God has heard our prayers. That does not mean we are not going to have bad days. I have to keep telling myself God knows we are human. He is God to comfort us, bless us, give us peace, and HEAL us.

We are so blessed by those who surround us. God has prepared us for this time in our lives. God prepared Trey from a very early age as is evident in some of the things he says. My earnest prayer is that God, in all His infinite wisdom, will allow Trey to be healed on earth. I want him to share His mighty works and what He has done for him; to go forward, spread His word and do His will as Christ did that long week before His crucifixion. God is receiving glory, but before all glory is received, there must be trials.

May you be blessed during this Easter week and seek the face of Jesus who saved us from our sins and gives us the faith we cling to each day.

April 4, 2012

Trey tweeted yesterday *"For what can be seen is temporary, but what cannot be seen is eternal ~ 2 Corinthians 4:18"*

Have you read the same thing over and over again and not thought anything about it? Then, read it again and a light bulb goes off? I think we do that with God's word, maybe a little too much!

We have been blessed by Martin Construction Company. They have come in and tiled our bathroom floor where we experienced a major flood and ruined our carpet. When Mark Martin walked in he said, "You don't remember me. I was the one here last year with your roof." Is God at work or what?

Over our bathtub is the scripture "With God All Things Are Possible". I'm not sure why I picked that out some years ago. Now, as Jay and I (and the children) walk in and out of that bathroom multiple times a day, God's word reminds me of His promise. This morning, I walked in and God spoke to me. I felt so convicted that I have His words on my wall, yet I take his promises so lightly.

And looking at them Jesus said to them, *"With people this is impossible, but with God all things are possible."* *Matthew 19:26*. This is not only in Matthew, but in Mark where it states "With GOD all things are possible." So where is our faith encouraged? Sometimes, it's from the bathroom wall. I know ALL things are possible for Trey.

To keep Trey's courage up, I texted him a verse:
LISA: ". . .watch and be utterly amazed. For I am going to do something in your day that you would not believe even if someone told you." Habakkuk 1:5 Love you."

TREY: "Wow that's a cool verse! Thanks! Love you too! Hope you have an easier work day today love you!" That would make any mother's day.

Trey has had a good couple of days. Saturday he walked. Sunday he walked. He has been to Taco Bell with his dad. Even on a good day, that's an accomplishment. We went to Julianne's house to watch the basketball game on Monday night. He gets tired very easily and does not last long, but he needs to be building up his strength. The next chemotherapy round is coming on Monday. My prayer is that he will feel well enough to attend church on Sunday for Easter. It's his goal also.

He has had calls this week from Inky Johnson and Carl Pickens, both Vols players at one time. They were very encouraging to him. Again, thanks to Phillip Fulmer for sending people Trey's direction to somehow relate and lift his spirits.

Before we headed out to watch the basketball game on Monday, we stopped at Walgreens to get some cough medicine for Trey. Yes, it's allergy season and he can only take a certain kind of cough medicine. When we were in the parking lot leaving, there was a small boy about 4 to 5 years of age with his mother.

"MOM, it's Trey. It's Trey Erwin!" the boy said waving, as hard as he could.

With Trey outside of his four walls, he saw what is happening in the community. Trey waved back and the mother and little boy and smiled. Trey thought that was the sweetest thing. I tell you this to encourage your little children to pray. They go before the Lord with eager, earnest pleas for a boy who they see is sick and a boy just like them. The Lord hears these children. It was Jesus who said in Luke 18:16:

"Permit the children to come to Me, and do not hinder them, for the kingdom of God belongs to such as these."

Trey tweeted today *"Certainly the LORD watches the whole earth carefully and is ready to strengthen those who are devoted to him. ~ 2 Chronicles 16:9"*

We have many prayer needs and our family is not ashamed to ask for those prayers. Trey will have a PET scan on Friday. We know the chemotherapy is working. It just has to be or his color would not be as good and he would not be feeling as good. Dr. Tauer at West Clinic told us that would be a sign the chemotheraphy would be working. Of course our prayer is the scan would show NO CANCER. Why can't it? With God all things are possible, right? But what if there is still cancer? Then we will go forward with whatever the plan Dr. Tauer and St. Jude has. We know it will be God's plan. HERE ME WHEN I SAY - WE KNOW THIS IS GOD'S PLAN. We have many people praying for us and that's where we would like for you to focus your prayers this week.

Thank you for your patience with our family. Please realize we don't sell the t-shirts from our home. We have had people show up to our door asking for t-shirts. Someone is taking care of this for us.

We hope you will continue to support our family in prayers and love. My boy sure needs it.

One year ago this month, we had an event at our church called Family of Families. The theme for the weekend was centered on building a firm foundation. During that time, we were encouraged to gather as a family, get a brick and write a scripture or word on it that we felt we should commit to in order to help us. Jay was at work, so we decided to bring the brick home and do this among the three of us. I knew I needed to work on being joyful, so I wrote JOY with

1 Corinthians 10: 13 *"No temptation has overtaken you but such as is common to man; and God is faithful, who will not allow you to be tempted beyond what you are able, but with the temptation will provide the way of escape also, so that you will be able to endure it."* Collin wrote LOVE with Job 34:19 *"Who shows no partiality to princes, Nor regards the rich above the poor, For they all are the work of His hands."* Trey wrote OBEY and chose Ephesians 6:1-3:

> *"Children, obey your parents in the Lord, for this is right. HONOR YOUR FATHER AND MOTHER (which is the first commandment with a promise), SO THAT IT MAY BE WELL WITH YOU, AND THAT YOU MAY LIVE LONG ON THE EARTH."*

At the time, he was dealing with so much. For him to step out in faith and accept his role of obedience was tremendous. Looking back I think God said, "Trey, you are ready. You are ready for the road you are about to travel." When he has a hard time accepting all of the blessings coming his way, I remind him of his great faithfulness to this verse.

Thursday night, we experienced the fundraiser at Incredible Pizza. Trey was very tired on Thursday and I wondered if we were even going to be able to make it. Jay and I talked all day about what it would be like if Trey didn't show up. At 4:30 p.m., he didn't want to get out of the bed and didn't know how he was going to get in the shower. I kept telling him we had to be at Incredible Pizza around 5:30 p.m. I was telling him just like I would be telling any normal teenager. Honestly, I was becoming a little exasperated.

I was downstairs and he urgently called for me. When I ran upstairs and said "WHAT?" he shoved his <u>Jesus Calling</u> book at me.

"Read this, read this!" he said.

As you go through this day, trust Me to provide the strength that you need moment by moment. Don't waste energy wondering whether you are adequate for today's journey. My Spirit within you is more than sufficient to handle whatever this day may bring.

"I gotta get in the shower. Let's blow this popsicle stand!" he continued.
I love to see God's hand at work in my son.

Trey met so many new friends at Incredible Pizza. He really had such a good time, but it wore him out. Not to minimize the University of Memphis Tigers - Antonio Anderson, Tarik Black, Preston Laird, D. J. Stephens and Coach Pastner's presence, but Trey's smile grew when he was in the middle of the University of Memphis Pom squad. After pictures, and more pictures, I was able to share a little of Trey's story with them. They are such sweet girls. One of them told me events like this were what she enjoyed most about being on the pom squad. Well, they made my boy happy. I wish so many of you could have seen Trey and Preston on the go cart track! We thank Incredible Pizza, the fire fighters, Sonya Luna, Lynne Berry, and many others. This could not have happened without their organization.

Julianne Shiles Thoughts: It was late at night and Trey and I were watching a movie. Trey was acting goofy on his meds and we decided to make an inspirational poster that he could put on the ceiling above his head. There was a fly buzzing around and it landed on the poster, so we decided to tape it to the poster and it's still there. The carpet had just been cleaned and Trey got frustrated with the glitter paint and squirted it to the point it got on the carpet. We knew we had messed up, but at 2 a.m. we didn't care because we had a good time.

April 6, 2012

In preparation for today's scan, Trey tweeted *"No matter the results, we will still praise you."* Sometimes I am in awe of his faith and have to ask if he's really mine! I have to beg for forgiveness for not having the faith that moves mountains like Trey does. Some days, it is just the size of a mustard seed.

The days that Trey goes to West Clinic are such a blessing. People will ask if I'm Trey's mom. Sometimes, I don't know whether to say yes or no. They are always so kind with encouraging words. Jay and Trey usually find a corner closest to the radiology entrance where they can compete on their phone playing the logo game. Trey cheats, so I always lose. Radiology is always good to get us back where Trey can lie down or, at least, get comfortable until his test.

PET scans are so important. Basically, all we are hoping for today are no new spots. When Dr. Tauer called, I held my breath. There are NO NEW SPOTS! We are very happy! This means all the time I worried about the cancer spreading to his stomach was for nothing. The three liver spots are still there but the pancreas has decreased in size slightly. All of this is very good. We will take it. Remember, he's only had two treatments. Dr. Tauer is very pleased and so are we. The chemotherapy is working. Progress! One step forward! Most of all, TREY was encouraged and decided to celebrate. So where do you go when you get good results of a PET scan? Trey goes to Waffle House, of course. If that doesn't go straight through him, I don't know what will.

Praise the LORD! And praise the Lord for waffles and movie nights with the family to celebrate!

April 9, 2012

Things change quickly. Trey didn't have a good night Friday night. It could have been the waffles. He woke up Saturday morning with a very bad headache, had nosebleeds during the night, and was running a fever. As far as the headaches, we know he deals with rebound headaches from the Dilaudid. I stayed home with Trey while Jay and Collin gathered with the family at his mother's for the Erwin Easter.

We have every kind of prescription medicine in the house, except Advil? Can you believe it? I can't express how blessed we are with friends. I was texting with my friend and joked about needing a giant bottle of Advil. Before I knew it, her son, and Trey's friend, Parks, was at our house with this HUGE bottle of Advil. After a few doses, Trey was able to sit up in bed, eat, and feel well enough to go eat a little at Granmaw's and have pictures made. He got to see family which was so important to Trey. He did not like missing the annual Easter egg hunt! Unfortunately, abdominal cramps hit and home we went.

Pain is what is prevents him from doing what he wants to do. He does not have his pain pump anymore so all pain medications is oral. Everything else goes through his Hickman line in his upper chest. I say the cramps stop him, but exhaustion is also a factor. My definition of exhaustion might be not feeling like going to the grocery store. Trey's definition of exhaustion is not having the strength to roll over in his bed. There are days and nights when it takes

~123~

everything he has to roll over. Those days come during chemotherapy, but they are coming more often now.

I knew he was not feeling good, so I woke up about 1:00 a.m. and went upstairs to check on him. Many nights, I have gone upstairs just to peek in on him. Tonight, he was fast asleep. As I came downstairs, I noticed our yard was brighter than usual, like there was a light in our front yard. I didn't have my glasses on, so I went to grab my glasses and my phone. When I looked outside, there was sign after sign of scripture in the yard. I just cried. I had no idea who came in the night to cover us in God's word. There were signs with scriptures he had tweeted, quotes from Jesus Calling, and many reminders of Trey's faithfulness and courage. Our family was in awe. So were the neighbors!

We planned, if he was feeling well, to go to the service Easter Sunday morning. About 7:30 a.m., his text read, I FEEL GREAT! Good enough for Sunday School! He wanted to make sure he looked nice, with a nice shirt and tie. We were able to go to Sunday School and to the church service. Seeing his friends in his worship comfort zone was such a blessing. After church, Trey said it was the best message he has heard. One thing we wrote down in our notes was God sets the parameters for death. Death does NOT have authority over God. Trey tweeted that later in the day. Jesus won that victory! Death is NOT something Trey is afraid of.

Just those few hours wore Trey out and he wanted to go home to bed. Later that afternoon he did get out for a walk, which he needed. Walking does help his cramps. (Also, he, Julianne, and Collin were able to get a little coloring in to put on the refrigerator. You are never too old to color.) Levsin also helps his cramps by relaxing the intestines and bladder. Jay and I have commented that we feel like we are reverting back to taking care of an infant. We would never tell Trey that! The cancer has caused his sleep patterns to reverse so he sleeps during the day and not at night. Many times when the chemotherapy side affects are hitting him the worst, he does not make it to the bathroom and we are up in the middle of the night washing his sheets, underwear. Sometimes, it happens multiple times during the night. He now has a satin pillow case so he can roll over easier and his hair will not pull out. Just as with infants, we deal with finding food his stomach will tolerate. It was easier feeding him formula. Then, there are the emotions caused by the drugs.

> **Julianne Shiles' Thoughts:** Trey and I had many things in common. One of the silly things was we loved to color. Easter Sunday afternoon we decided we didn't have enough coloring books so we raided Walmart. Trey picked out Toy Story and I picked out The Little Mermaid. We also bought a stuffed Simba and Nala from The Lion King. Their noises stick together by a magnet. We spent the afternoon coloring. We taped the pictures on the refrigerator. We colored a lot while he was sick. I think it made him feel better.

Today, we went to West Clinic to see Dr. Tauer and for his third chemotherapy treatment. I have learned to be prepared before seeing the doctors. Once I am with them, I forget my questions. This was today's list:
*If you were treating an older man, how would he compare at this stage to Trey? He said Trey is doing excellent.
*What do we do about Trey's nosebleeds? Dr. Tauer said chemotherapy causes the lining of the nose to thin. Trey needs to use a little vaseline to coat his nose to cut down

on the nosebleeds. Trey has always had nosebleeds but now they last for longer periods of time.

*How are Trey's counts? They are still good. He is a little anemic and his platelets are slightly low, but overall they are still stable. This will account for him being so tired.

*How many treatments is he going to have? Dr. Tauer does not know. We are looking at this in three week increments. In four weeks he will have a CT scan. Since he has had a PET scan, he will only need a CT scan.

*What about the future treatment options we talked about? Dr. Tauer said he would not need to be drastically better in order to do the liver ablation which he would do first. This procedure would be done on Trey because his liver lesions are so small and Dr. Tauer said he may be able to reduce the size even more. This is not to say it will be done soon. But there would need to be change in order for him to proceed with this procedure.

*When will he get his Hickman line changed to a port in order to go to Hawaii? Dr. Tauer told us Dr. Hodgkiss only needs about 4 days. We will wait until right before we go to get this done.

*Are we all clear to travel to the University of Tennessee for the weekend? We have to make sure we see Dr. Sara and Karen Williams at St. Jude before we go to get his counts checked. We go to St. Jude on April 18 and fly out on a private plane on April 20 for the Orange and White game.

*Dr. Tauer asked if Trey was always this out of it? Does he ever have alert, awake moments? I was glad Dr. Tauer was seeing Trey in this state. This is the way he is during the day and it has worried me a little. But we did tell him, absolutely, there are times he has energy. We told him he had a very long weekend and was very tired. Trey was totally zoned out and could not hold his eyes open.

*We asked Dr. Tauer about Trey's abdominal cramps. He said to stop the Creon because the cramps are a precursor to diarrhea and to continue the Levsin. We can even take a half a Levsin during the middle of the day. The only bad side effect from the Levsin is blurred vision and he is not able to read. If the Levsin is working for the cramps, he can handle a little blurred vision.

Dr. Tauer was very pleased with Trey's progress. Could it have been better? Of course. He said we can go one of three ways - get better, stay stable, or get worse. Only time and Trey's body will tell.

Trey is continuing with school, even during days he has chemotherapy. That's very difficult. It's very hard for him to focus and he gets frustrated. Dr. Sara told said, if we had an obsessive compulsive child prior to cancer, steroids will increase that problem. So, Trey is bothered by getting his work done, keeping his room clean and, even the medicines on his dresser. We are told this will get better. Trey has the remote to his television, his phone, his bible, his devotion book, Jesus Calling, and his other devotion book close to him. He won't allow anyone to sit on the end of his bed because it might wrinkle the blanket on his bed and the one folded at the foot. All of his shirts, pants, and shorts are hung in his closet grouped in colors with all his Polo clothing together. He is obsessed with doing his laundry, usually around 2 a.m. Some think this is a blessing! If I could loan him out to do your laundry, I would. Fortunately, one thing we taught Trey before cancer was how to do his own laundry. He has had no problem with this set up and neither have we!

Jay is still at home with Trey every day. What a blessing it has been to have the fire department cover his shifts. Collin is doing very well. He starts band practice after school on every Tuesday for the next few weeks, so he will be busy. I am still working until 3 p.m. each day, but will be working on getting my desk in order to start my family medical leave soon. Trust me, we have good days and bad days, just like everyone else! Thank goodness for a loving, merciful God.

God continues to open doors. I am sure he has closed doors along the way, but I have not seen those because he opens another door so quickly. It would be easy to let Satan send doubts our way and question every step. That would go against everything God has taught us, though, as parents. If we've ever needed to be examples of Christ to our children, it is now.

"My heart is confident in you, O God, my heart is confident. No wonder I can sing your praises!" Psalms 57:7

April 11, 2012

I think last night was the worst night we have had. Every time he has a bad night I say that, but it seems they do get worse. Trey threw up every couple of hours. At first, he said it was the Taco Bell he had from lunch. That was at 7 p.m. Then he said it was the pizza. You have got to love boys. Just admit it son! The chemotherapy is kicking your tail this time!

We gave him every nausea medication we had and it still didn't keep him down. At least he gets his chemotherapy pump off today at West Clinic. The sensitivity to cold has really kicked in too. He is wearing gloves because his fingers are tingling. He needs good rest!

Certainly, all this has affected his social life. He is attached to his phone, so try to not text him for just a little while. Pick it up later this afternoon. He will not like that I said that!

Jim Siegfried came to see us at West Clinic on Monday. He said something so wise. Since he has traveled down this treacherous road, he should know. He said our body does its best healing while it is sleeping. That's why Trey needs to sleep and not just nap. What a blessing Jim is to our family. He has come so far with his own cancer and I know his heart poured out for Trey. Jim baptized Trey when he was 8 years old. Jim, Cyndi, Tara, Cade, Cade (Jr.), Corbin, and Quinn, we love your family! Actually, it is very humorous when Jim comes to see Trey at West Clinic. We never know who he will tell them he is - a relative, a church friend, etc. He has been there with Trey for treatments, procedures, and helping us understand our walk through this disease.

We covet your prayers as we get over this hump this week. I left Jay in the recliner in Trey's room and told Trey if he needed mama to come home, just call. Do you really think I'm going to get anything done today?

God led me to a new friend in San Antonio last night through the internet. She heard of Trey's story. I enjoyed our talk and everything we shared. I love having new sisters in the Lord to help us through this new normal.

CHAPTER 12

NEW GOALS AND LIMITS

"Commit your way to the LORD, Trust also in Him,
and He will do it." Psalms 37:5

April 12, 2012

When I got home yesterday afternoon, Trey was not feeling better. He had not been out of bed all day. When I say he had not been out of bed, I mean, he had not been out of bed to even go to the bathroom.

He was very lethargic and his temp was 100.1. Granted, that is below the temp required for admittance to St. Jude, but he had so many other things going on, including having thrown up most of the night. I knew something else was wrong! As I was driving up to my house, God had Dr. Sara send me a text checking on him. When I reported back to her, she called me and decided it would be best to pack some bags and take him to St. Jude.

We knew he would need fluids, which they immediately hung. They also checked his counts. He received an antibiotic to cover his fever. His white count was low, but not dangerously low. His potassium was low. His platelets and hemoglobin were normal. That is good! He got through one liter of fluids and Dr. Sara decided to send us home with a second bag of fluids. Trey was so happy he didn't have to stay. He just wanted to come home to his bed, even though he didn't feel good.

This round of chemotherapy was so much harder on him than the first two rounds and his body was not ready for it. He is on schedule with his chemotherapy, but his body is weak. Dr. Sara changed around some of his medications to make him more comfortable and be able to function. He was able to get IV Phenergan last night and, immediately, went to sleep. That gave Jay and I time to talk to Dr. Sara about details we had not had time to discuss since his diagnosis a month ago.

I think since things have sunk in, I still wanted to ask the same questions. So many people have talked to us about being in remission, cures, etc. from pancreatic cancer. Dr. Sara confirmed, unless the Lord heals, there is no such thing for pancreatic adenocarcinoma! It was disheartening to hear she didn't recommend surgery on the pancreas. Trey's cancer is in the head of the pancreas where most of the plumbing for the stomach and liver runs. It is such a risky surgery and this cancer has already spread. It will continue to spread even when the tumor in the pancreas is gone. Trey has asked the same questions. We have been told the tumor probably started in the duodenum and grew into the head of the pancreas. That's the reason it would be such a difficult surgery. Not only that, Trey would have to survive the surgery and the difficult recovery time. Dr. Sara knew the question before I even asked. Even if it was successful, the surgery would not add any time to Trey's life. Most of my questions were for a surgeon to answer. I will ask those questions of a surgeon, but we need to get better quality of life for Trey first. There is no way he could make it through a surgery at this point. He is too sick.

God is faithful and He continues to speak to us. We gave Trey over to God as a small child to use as He wished. When this started, I did it again. It's so hard not to tell God I want to keep him! Please just let me keep him. And God sends this to me this morning:

> *"Let us hold tightly without wavering to the hope we affirm, for God can be trusted to keep his promise." Hebrews 10:23*

Please pray for us as we continue to hold tightly. Thank you for your encouragement.

There are a number of events going on in April...

*On Saturday, April 14, there is a Prowler Push-a-thon at NBS Fitness from 10 to 1 at 564 Trinity Creek Cove in Cordova.

*On Tuesday, April 17, there is the big Collierville v. Houston lacrosse game at Collierville. We will be attending the varsity game at 8 p.m. Come support the team of your choice. Of course, we will be supporting our Dragons!

*Zumbathon is on Friday, April 20, at 6:30 p.m. at Victory University which is located on N. Highland. Channel 5 will be covering this event.

*On Saturday, April 28, there will be a benefit show at Grace Evan for Trey, originally scheduled for this Friday.

*Mama Mia Pizza is the old Johnny Bruscos. They have offered to donate a portion of what they take in to our family. So please feel free to visit Mama Mia's from April 16-30. Great Pizza!

I cannot wait for Fair on the Square in Collierville and to have Tailgate for the Cure to be here with their booth set up to support Trey and St. Jude. Come out May 5-7.

Continue to pray for Trey's strength as we plan for two trips. On April 20, we fly to Knoxville for the Orange and White game and May 6, we leave for our Make a Wish trip to Hawaii. Both of these trips are very important to Trey and he will need all the strength he can muster to have a good time.

Before he went to bed tonight, I sent him a text, "I want you to read John 15:16 before you go to bed and remember what we, as Christians, are all about. I am very proud of you and love you very much."

"You didn't choose Me but I chose you, and appointed you that you would go and bear fruit, and your fruit would

remain, so that whatever you ask of the Father in My name He may give to you."- John 15:16

TREY: "Wow very powerful thank you mom love you lots too."

Trey then tweeted *"God sets the parameters for death, death does not have authority over God @charlesafowler"* Thank you for letting Trey rest this week. We could not survive without the community support!

April 15, 2012

Trey's tweet for April 13 was *"Happy birthday S/O to @LisaErwin13! She is the BEST mom anyone could ask for I love her so much! For every thing you do mom, I love you!!!"*

It is April 13, my birthday. I would love to spend my birthday at home and have a quiet evening. But, Collierville High School planned a dance with a portion of the proceeds going to the Pray for Trey account and Trey wanted to make an appearance. Most of the teenagers don't start their evening until 9 p.m. or later, so Trey didn't want to show up to the high school until at least 9 p.m. So, for my birthday, I received the best present I could ask for - a date with my son to a high school dance.

When we arrived, there was not a huge crowd and Trey tweeted *"Everybody come to the Collierville main gym!!! Now!!"* I watched Trey talk with friends, smile, and pace back and forth, which usually meant he was hurting. We waited for friends to come to the gym and, eventually, headed home. As we were in the parking lot to leave, friends began to arrive and tweet him asking if he was still there. He had to call it a night. He enjoyed seeing his friends and I know he wished more had been there, but he was glad to be able to go to school. I was glad to have a handsome date for my birthday!

Remember when a "C" was average? I think parents today look at a "C" as an "F", like 60 is the new 40. What happened to just being average? Why do so many people push their children to be overachievers? Trust me, I'm going somewhere with this "average".

It has really been a tough week for Trey, the third week of chemotherapy. It hit him like a ton of bricks. If he does not gain strength, the chemotherapy will continue to bring him down physically and mentally.

One day this week, Trey was in excruciating pain. He has lost so much weight, his hips are very boney. It helps his stomach to lie on one side in one position. This day, he rolled over. Yes, that is it. He rolled over. Like a baby, that was the accomplishment for the day. He was so weak, but so glad he could get from one side to the other. My sister, Donna, and best friend, Cindy Few, made sure he had an egg crate on his mattress, which has helped tremendously. What a major goal for his day! So simple, yet average.

Average describes our family. Right now, our phone rings, the doorbell rings, and the cell phone dings constantly. Most of the time, it's people we don't even know. We go to church and see one, ten, twenty people we normally would not see and update them on the status of Trey and the family. We go to the grocery, the pharmacy, WalMart, even Best Buy and people tell us they are praying for our family, especially when we are sitting at West Clinic. We cannot personally acknowledge and thank everyone like we would like to. I was overwhelmed just by the sheer number of birthday wishes I received on Facebook! I cannot imagine how Trey feels. I know he feels a little of "why me?" since there are so many others that are sick too.

Trey has so many people following him on Twitter, his favorite social network. When the Lord speaks to him, which he says is usually early in the morning when he cannot sleep, he may tweet a verse. He is amazed people will respond at how inspirational he is when all he is doing is putting a verse on Twitter. We are setting a goal to understand, one day at a time, how to continue strengthening our faith. We all need to do that as a family. We don't need to worry about tomorrow, for tomorrow will take care of itself. We are not going to talk about how much time is left. We are going to concentrate on the time today.

Trey tweeted today *"Being blessed by Jesus is so overwhelming I can't even put it into words #indescribable"*

As Pastor Charles prayed with me today, he shared a scripture passage that spoke to me of how Jehoshaphat cried out to the Lord to deliver him and his people. In verses 20-22 it says:

> *"Listen to me, Judah and people of Jerusalem! Have faith in the LORD your God and you will be upheld; have faith in his prophets and you will be successful." After consulting the people, Jehoshaphat appointed men to sing to the LORD and to praise him for the splendor of his holiness as they went out at the head of the army, saying:*
> *"Give thanks to the LORD, for his love endures forever." As they began to sing and praise, the LORD set ambushes against the men of Ammon and Moab and Mount Seir who were invading Judah, and they were defeated." 2 Chronicles 20:19-22*

We are fighting a war against cancer. Our battles are many. Our goal is to praise the Lord everyday and experience *"as they sang praise, the Lord drove the enemy out."* We can give praise for the situation we are in, for the lives being changed, for the people providing for us, for everyone giving of their time to help us, for the doctors and their knowledge and so many other things. Be thankful with us.

This morning, Trey sent me a text and asked what the game plan was. I told him, unless he was able to go to Sunday School, we would just go to church. He said he could go to church. We got ready and started to leave. As I was getting everyone out the door, he said he was just too tired to go. I sent him back to bed.

Before cancer, we would have attended Sunday School and worship and been back to youth choir at 4:00, Project 22 (bible study), and evening worship at 6 p.m. Normally, I would be vibrating in the kitchen if we were not walking out the door on time. Now, things are quite different. If we make it to ONE service, I am thankful to be at worship. God knows our limits. When we are weak, He is strong. We know He will sustain us.

Trey is now more conscientious about taking his medications before he leaves the house. He will send me a text asking me to set the Zofran out. Nausea medication is a must if he is going to church. He tries to take notes, talk to people, take pictures and, frankly, do more than he should.

This particular Sunday, it was hard for him to keep his laughter under control. Julianne was assigned a baby to keep for a weekend as part of a class at Houston High School. During the middle of the service, the baby started crying and Julianne had to leave the service multiple times. We could not help but laugh at the way Julianne would grab the baby by the neck! Trey sent me a text, "Ha I feel sorry for the baby! At least I'm not the one getting the grade." I am not so sure he was able to concentrate during this service because he started getting hungry. When his stomach begins to cramp, it means he needs to eat. It's the same as my stomach growling. The only difference is his cramps turn into excruciating pain. Sonic after church it is!

Trey even went to Under Authority today (Youth Choir). He left the room and I had to send him a text to ask him if he was okay. He answered me and said he was tired, but he felt fine and needed to take his pants off because they were feeling a little tight. He does not need anything to bring on cramps.

I'm proud of Trey being able to tell his friends he needs rest, but it has been so hard for him to do. He misses being with his friends, but he knows he needs to gain his strength. We want Trey to gain strength not cancer cells!

Average? Yes, we are an average family who loves the Lord. We have struggled this week, cried this week, turned to our Pastor, been to St. Jude, unexpectedly, and zapped with chemotherapy. Jay and I are nursing a teenager with terminal cancer while trying to raise Collin in the most normal environment as possible. It would be easy to say to someone, walk in my shoes just 24 hours and your life would change, but we know average in today's world equals stress. Average equals a "C". God loves the average. And I praise him among the stress this week as we have cried out, He still loves us.

> "O Lord, my God, I cried to Thee for help, and Thou didst heal me." Psalms 30:2

Trey *tweeted "…I will strengthen you, surely I will help you, surely I will uphold you with My righteous right hand.-Isaiah 41:10"*

CHAPTER 13

KNOXVILLE! GO BIG ORANGE!

"I committed my life to Christ, and that faith has been most important to me ever since."
Peyton Manning

April 19, 2012

What a full week Trey has had. Wait. What a full week we ALL have had. It is so true his strength has come from the Lord. He has had his days and night mixed up and has contributed to his fatigue. There are many other things that have contributed, but not being able to sleep is a major factor. He tries and we have so many medications we are giving him, but they just are not working the way we are giving them to him. We hope all of that is going to change!

A friend from church contacted us about filming a short faith story with our family in conjunction with the premier of the Victor Marx Movie being shown at Highpoint. Kyle and Stacie Munyon told us Germantown Baptist and Highpoint were sponsoring the premiere and, in conjunction with the event, wanted to take donations for our family. Our faith story would play before the movie. For months, I've wondered if I could capture what we were experiencing. God put Kyle and Stacie, Grant Guffin, Flashlight Media, and Josh Maze in our laps.

Convincing Trey of the potential impact took a little explaining because his mind isn't always totally clear. He was willing, as long as someone prompted him. I prayed he would be of clear mind and feeling strong for days before the actually filming.

Monday, Grant Guffin and his video company came to our house for the taping along with Stacie Munyon. It was a fun process and a special time for our family. We were able to make fun of Trey and, of course, he made fun of us. I am so proud of Collin. My little fidget did so well. Now, when someone asks, we will be able to share a DVD of where our journey started. I have not seen the final product and honestly, I am kind of scared. Who likes to see themselves on video? They say the camera makes you look 10 pounds heavier. Trey can use that, I cannot!

Trey seemed like a professional! It came straight from his heart. As he was talking, I saw Jay looking out the front door. Hearing his son talk about his own illness bothered him.

Trey said exactly what he had been putting on social media. *"I'm not doing anything but sending out a tweet from a bible verse I read that day. And all the glory goes to God in everything. I'm not inspiring anybody. I'm being used by God. I just want all the glory to go to Him and none, none, none to me."* Well said, buddy. Well said.

After we finished taping, one of his buddies from Kid's Worship at church came to visit. Trey misses his kids so much! Trey had such a good time visiting with Noah Delk. Jack Green has been by twice. The little boys just love Trey and he loves them. Leading in Kid's Worship is one of the things he misses most about church. But he says he will be back soon. I think the children are counting on it!

On Tuesday, we were able to participate in the Collierville/Houston Lacrosse game and Trey served as an honorary captain. Even though he wore one of the jerseys with the #13 of a team member, he loved the coin they gave him after the coin toss. The crowd that came out for the game was unbelievable. Lacrosse is the new popular sport to play, not to mention there is a huge rivalry between Collierville and Houston in ANY sport. Trey was able to see so many of his friends. And, the smile on his face did his mom and dad some good. But he didn't last long. We were at the field by 7:15 p.m. and needed to leave by 8:30 p.m. The only comfortable position for him is standing but he cannot stand for very long. BIG shout out to Collierville High School and Houston High School for supporting us during this game. Steve Shipowitz, you are a hero and a wonderful coach of these Collierville boys. For two rival schools to come together to support Trey touched our hearts. I believe it touched the entire community too.

This morning, we had a visit to St. Jude. This was only our second scheduled appointment at St. Jude to go through the process of talking with all the different doctors, departments, etc. If you are a St. Jude parent, you know exactly what I am talking about. These visits are an all day process. At registration, we picked up a printout of appointments for the day. Then, we just follow the schedule in order, not necessarily on time.

After three rounds of chemotherapy, Trey's counts are good. Even though it was day 9 or so after chemotherapy, it should be when his counts would be at the bottom starting to trend up. There was nothing out of the ordinary to be alarmed about.

One concern is his fatigue. He's now started Ritalin to give him a boost of energy and strength during the day (but he won't share). It will help him stay awake during the day and, hopefully, will help when he actually needs to get some sleep at night. I don't foresee having a problem with him being overactive.

He's also started Elavil for several reasons - weight gain, sleep, mood stabilizer, and pain. The main reason for the Elavil is to help with his being so obsessive compulsive. I am thankful he washes his own clothes and wants to put them up. As I mentioned before, I only wish he wouldn't do it at 2 a.m. We are also using a phone app called HeyTell. I get a HeyTell message from Trey around midnight.

TREY: "Hey, will someone bring up my clean clothes out of the dryer so I can fold them? I don't want them to get wrinkled." (speech slurred)

Trey has also started Emend, another nausea drug. Honestly, I've lost count of how many nausea medications he's taking! This one will only be administered during chemotherapy and we will not have any responsibility of administering it.

Since Trey had such a bad experience with his last chemotherapy treatment, Dr. Sara has decided he will receive fluids 24 hours prior to chemotherapy, all during chemotherapy, and then 24 hours after chemotherapy on Mondays. That means he will start a bag of fluids on Sunday night. Hopefully, he'll stay hydrated and not be as nauseated.

We talked to the dietitian because we are all are concerned about his weight loss. He's definitely eating, but his body is not absorbing the caloric intake. Trey has now lost 30 pounds. That is approximately 15% of his body weight. He is going to go back on TPN, but only at night. To do this, after Trey has chemotherapy on Monday, we will check into St. Jude so the TPN can be started again. The admission is a precaution against refeeding syndrome. Patients who develop refeeding syndrome are potentially susceptible to pulmonary, cardiac, neuromuscular, and hematologic complications. Combined with the weight loss, restarting the TPN could make Trey very sick and get his counts and electrolytes out of balance. So, we are killing two birds with one stone. He will get his last part of his chemotherapy from his pump at St. Jude and have the TPN started at the same time. If he gets sick, he will be at the most awesome place to take care of him. He says that's where the best looking nurses are! Hey, he is a boy after all. Finally, while we are there, his Hickman line will be converted to a portacath so he can swim when we go to Hawaii.

We found out today how he contracted his cancer. Trey agreed to genetic testing early in the journey. He did test positive for a p16 mutation, something found in many cancers, most often melanoma. Pancreatic adenocarcinoma is associated with mutations in the p16 gene. St. Jude is taking many steps right now and has called the National Cancer Institute to follow up on Trey's genetic testing. This gene is passed from parent to child. When we heard this news, Jay immediately turned to the wall and could not face Trey. Dr. Sara tried to reassure Jay and my first thought went to Collin. Now, we are trying to be proactive concerning research in this matter. It is like putting a puzzle together. Jay's brother, Barry, and Jay's dad, Jerry, have all had melanoma. Now, it makes sense. The gene is so strong in Trey's DNA, even at age 15.

We left St. Jude on that note with plans in place for our next move. Trey tweeted after our St. Jude visit, *"Blessed are those who have been persecuted for the sake of righteousness, for theirs is the kingdom of heaven. Matthew 5:10"*

On a happier note, did you know the Grizzlies are headed to the playoffs? Well, we do! Just ask Trey. He could have told you last night from the locker room. I cannot begin to tell you what an experience it was for Jay, Trey, Julianne and I to sit in Chris Wallace's seats and watch the game! Trey talked non-stop about his experience in the locker room. When he walked back in the sandwich room, he came in with Rudy Gay's shoes (uh, boats, sorry Rudy), we just died! Rudy gave him his shoes and signed them. And the whole team passed a ball around and signed it. He told us how he was in the locker room with the guys walking around without towels like it was nothing to them. We had a lot of good laughs. Trey and Julianne also got their picture with Tony Allen. It was first class treatment by Mr. Wallace as Trey toured the facilities of the Forum. Chris Wallace, General Manager of the Grizzlies is a class act!

Trey tweeted with a picture, *"good seats to grizz game or what?"*

Friday afternoon, Collierville High School held a special pep rally for Trey. When we walked into a gym full of students, there were ERWIN 13, "We got your back", and "Pray for Trey" t-shirts everywhere. All of our family was there. Tears welled in my eyes as I saw the larger than life football poster of Trey on the gym wall with Pray for Trey printed on it. I just knew he was going to walk out of poster and into the slim body standing in the middle of the gym floor! Members of the Collierville City Council and Mayor Stan Joyner were there. Trey was presented a proclamation by the Mayor naming July 31, 2012, as Trey Erwin Day.

Thanks to Balfour, Trey was the first sophomore to receive his class ring. Everyone wanted to see Trey's ring, including the media in attendance. At one point, I counted three microphones in his face at the same time.

There were so many posters, gifts and honors! Trey was overwhelmed, especially by the Grizz girls who presented Trey with an ERWIN Grizzlies jersey signed by all the team members. My heart began to drop as I watched him mingle among his friends and sit on the bleachers with his classmates and his football team. There he sat, so comfortable with Isaiah and Corbin, with no complaint of not feeling good.

When Trey left the gym full of the people he loved, he tweeted *"Ya'll are amazing. I am so blessed to have support from ya'll #loveyouguys #CHS"* I could not have said it better.

As much as we hated to leave the pep rally, we had a plane to catch for the next most exciting thing Trey can experience! We are to board a private jet at 4:30 p.m. to fly to Knoxville, Tennessee, for the Orange and White game. We will fly back on a private jet on Sunday.

"Give ear to my words, O Lord, consider my sighing. Listen to my cry for help, my King and my God, for to you I pray. In the morning, O Lord, you hear my voice; in the morning I lay my requests before you and wait in expectation." Psalms 5:1-3

April 24, 2012

Tonight in the St. Jude cafeteria, I found myself humming, randomly. Then I was singing. My kids hate it when I do that! I never know why these songs, like The Doxology, come to mind when they do.

Praise God, from whom all blessings flow;

Praise Him, all creatures here below;

Praise Him, above ye heavenly host;

Praise Father, Son, and Holy Ghost.
Amen.

So many people asked us to describe explain how we felt about everything that happened in order to get us to Knoxville. I wish I could have just sung The Doxology as an answer. Too many things fell into place for God's hand to not be directly touching everything each step of the way.

Trey tweeted, *"Just landed in Knoxville! #soexcited"*
This weekend would not have happened without the direct involvement of Amanda Johnson Weeks-Geveden. She did

~144~

an amazing job arranging private planes, hotel, food, car rentals, and all kinds of goodies when we arrived at the hotel. When we walked into the hotel room, Trey's face lit up when he saw Eric Berry's jersey hanging and signed to Trey. There were t-shirts, books from Inky Johnson, mini helmets, and many other University of Tennessee goodies.

The tradition of the rock is very important at the University of Tennessee. A large rock on the campus and is painted at least once every 24 hours. As a surprise for Trey, some of the college kids from our church (Morgan, Karson, Cole, Julia, and Jessica) painted the rock for Trey. Our first stop after getting settled at the hotel, and getting over the shock of the signed Eric Berry jersey, was the rock. What an amazing sight! It said – Welcome Erwins #Pray for Trey, with the purple pancreatic cancer ribbon in the background and Trey's Caringbridge site address. And it got the word out in Knoxville! We spent an hour climbing all over the rock taking pictures. Trey didn't do any climbing, but I know he wanted to try. It will be painted over within hours, but it's something special to be a Tennessee fan and have your name painted on the rock. Trey's face hurt from smiling and being with his friends.

On Saturday, the Young Alumni Association at the University of Tennessee recognized Trey as a "young alumnus" for the day. Eric Haag, Director of Alumni Programs, made that possible as well as scheduling our entire day. He contacted Knoxville Channel 10 news and arranged for Mary Scott, news anchor, to follow us all day. She was so kind and said she would have a video of the day for us to keep.

Bad weather threatened and Trey didn't have much energy when he got up that morning. Friday took so much energy out of him and he didn't have time to rest. So, we took a van to the tours and, later, to the stadium.

After lunch, Eric took us to the stadium and we talked with Chris Fuller who I had been talking with on the phone in the athletic department. Chris introduced us to Brad Pendergrass, Director of Football Operations. Brad was wonderful to Trey and our family. He took Trey into the locker room where Trey was able to take pictures and talk with Tyler Bray, Justin Hunter, DaRick Rogers and many others. He also met and talked with Coach Derek Dooley. We loved it when Coach Dooley came out of the locker room asking, "Where's mom and dad?" He insisted on pictures with the family and knew why we were there.

I wish I could have captured Trey's face when we walked onto the field. The only way it could have been better would have been to be walking through the T!!! The awesomeness of standing in the stadium where he dreamed of playing in was overwhelming for Trey. I cannot describe what my heart was feeling every time he would say or someone would say to him "You'll be back here in two years on this field".

Brad grabbed a game ball, gave it to Trey and gave Tyler a shout. He came over and started throwing with Trey. I took a deep breath. If I had not been taking pictures, I would have cried. I was watching him live his dream! I know it felt good for Trey to throw the ball again. More than that, he was throwing with the quarterback of the University of Tennessee IN Neyland Stadium. And, no, he never dropped a pass!

As people began to fill the stadium, I heard our names called. There were friends from Memphis in the stands, cheering as Trey threw the ball. I know it was only by God's strength he was able to throw the ball at all. Afterwards, I asked him how he was able to do it. He told me he honestly didn't know. Adrenaline can be your friend at times.

He tweeted, *"Just played catch with Tyler Bray #overwhelmed"*

I know it was hard for Trey to leave the field. He knew he would not be back in two years, but he lived a dream today. We proceeded to our box seats and relaxed to watch what the Vols were going to be all about during the 2012 season.

Sometimes it is the little things in life. Trey ate a steak dinner. Amanda arranged for us to have dinner at Ruth's Chris after the game. I think Trey would say the meal was worth it, even though it kept him up most of the night. I don't think he could have taken enough enzymes to reduce the fat and grease in that steak! I don't remember hearing him calling my name until, probably, the third time he was in the bathroom. After I heard him calling, I was able to help him get as many medications down as he could to settle his digestive tract.

Four of us were stuck in one room and laughter commenced at Trey's expense. Trey was laughing too because there was no way to escape the smell. Trey travels with his Hawaiian floral deodorizer spray because he thinks that will make it better. Trey took the blame because he could not stay out of the bathroom. On Sunday, we flew home to reality to pack for St. Jude for a week.

Trey received chemotherapy at West Clinic yesterday. Immediately afterwards, we left for St. Jude (aka the Jude). Trey's put the St. Jude logo on Instagram with the caption *"Back at my second home"*. This was a planned visit to restart his TPN. His body does not absorb the nutrients from his food so he continues to lose weight, no matter what he eats. He will only be receiving the TPN at night. This way, he will keep his appetite during the day along with the steroids he is receiving.

Here I am again, in a dark room with my son hooked up to tubes. Thankfully, he is sleeping.   On Thursday, the Hickman line will be removed and he'll get the portacath. This will make him feel so much better! He won't have to be bandaged to take a shower and it gets us one step closer to Hawaii.

We are scheduled to go home from the Jude on Friday. Keith Cochran came by today with a stack of cards that had been mailed to the church. I had to read most of them to him because he was so sleepy. They were such a blessing! Most of the cards and letters began, *"You don't know me, but..."* We were amazed.

Jay is going to work a few hours at Baptist ER tomorrow. That's a very big blessing. Sometimes, we need to focus on other things to keep our mind fresh. I can't help but worry about my own job.   Even with all the support and reassurance, Jay and I realize the corporate world may not hold my job forever and we may be required to make tough decisions.

No matter what, Trey will come first. We have been faithful to give God glory and acknowledge Him in this journey.   I know He will take care of us. Knowing that doesn't mean it is not a little scary, but God never promised it would be easy.

Trey brought his bible to the Jude with this scripture underlined. I think it describes Trey, our family, and what we are trying to live each day. Can I just say, I am so proud of my son?

> *"Be joyful always; pray continually; give thanks in all circumstances, for this is God's will for you in Christ Jesus." 1 Thessalonians 5:16*

CHAPTER 14

NOW JUST WAIT A MINUTE!

"Cast all your anxiety on him because he cares for you."
1 Peter 5:7

April 26, 2012

What a day! More specifically, what a night and day! Trey's day started about 2:30 a.m. when he woke me up and said he thought he was going to be sick. Then, he got sick. That continued on and off until 10 a.m. this morning. He also had a low grade fever.

We THOUGHT Trey was scheduled to have his portacath installed at 1 p.m. Around 8:15 a.m., the nurse came in and told us he was going at 8:30. I called Jay, and reached him as he was arriving at the Jude. Then, hold everything! They decided to move him to the end of the schedule to give his body time to settle down. It had been a long night and he was not ready for a procedure of any kind. After he got sick around 10 a.m., the doctors postponed the procedure again. They didn't want to take a chance of him aspirating in the operating room. We all agreed this was best for Trey.

Trey is so weak, at this point, he does not care. He just wants to sleep. I want to know how Trey got so sick, so fast? As a mama, I want to know why and I want to know now. More importantly, I want it fixed. And, I want someone held accountable because he was fine. Those are questions I may not ever get the answers to. The final answer was a combination of reasons - getting behind on a round of pain and nausea medication, chemotherapy, and/or TPN. Am I supposed to be okay with that?

Even knowing it was possible didn't make it less frightening to see Trey so lethargic. All day, the doctors and nurses worked to find the right combination of pain and nausea medications for him. About 1 p.m., I decided I had to step outside. I went down the street to my office, greasy hair, too big sweat pants, no make-up and all! Not to mention, I had lost track of the last time I had showered. With a sick child constantly calling out, a shower was the last thing on my mind.

I came back from my office to find Trey and Jay resting, such a comforting sight. I think I needed a break more than I realized. When Jay was leaving to go home tonight I told him I was tired of having to be strong. I just get weary.

Sometimes I feel like crying shows physical weakness and it also shows weakness in faith. When I shared this with my Pastor, he reminded me that Jesus had emotions. Jesus cried. The story of Lazarus' death, told in John 11, shows how upset Jesus was when he saw Mary weeping.

"Therefore, when Mary came where Jesus was, she saw Him, and fell at His feet, saying to Him, "Lord, if You have been here, my brother would not have died." When Jesus therefore saw her weeping, and the Jews who came with her also weeping, He was deeply moved in spirit and was troubled, and said, "Where have you laid him?" They said to Him, "Lord come and see." Jesus wept. So the Jews were saying, "See how He loved him!" John 11:32-36

I sat and looked at Trey today in the bed. It brought back familiar memories. Memories I would rather not have. I turned and picked up Jesus Calling and read:

Circumstances are in flux, and the world is spinning around you. The only way to keep your balance is to fix your eyes on Me, the One who never changes. If you gaze too long at your circumstances, you will become dizzy and confused!

That is so true. Today, when I was walking from the cafeteria at dinner, I felt like all the paintings on the wall were closing in on me. I can see it on Jay's face when he is not holding up well. Trey's weakened state hurts us. I read a commentary today called "What is Faith Like?" There are two sides of faith, assurance and expectation. The commentary said: "Ultimately, the way we see God will determine the shape of our faith. If we see a big, faithful, all-powerful God, then our faith will rise to those levels. If, on the other-hand, we see a smaller God, a less distant or less active God, then faith will plateau at those levels."
"Now faith is being sure of what we HOPE for and CERTAIN of what we do not see." Hebrews 11:1
I want to be known to have BIG faith, not wavering or small - a cancer conquering faith, I want a faith that looks doubt in the face and says "You have no hold over me. I CAN cry because God is in control!" If I know Trey like I think I do, he would want that too!

April 28, 2012

Trey's procedure went fine. They installed a double port which will help when he has multiple medications that are not compatible. We are increasing our prayer requests. Trey is very nauseated. His sodium has dropped and they are going to tweak this in his TPN. Jay stayed with him last night so I could come home for a night. I am getting some important things done, like my toes, and will go back to St. Jude for the night. Getting my toes done doesn't fix anything but it definitely helps my outlook!

We need to see Trey more awake, eating, and taking medications by mouth, not to mention the normal things like walking and going to the bathroom. Trey has not done any texting or tweeting. We know he does not feel good when he does not look at his phone. He physically cannot pick it up and look at it.

We leave one week from tomorrow for Hawaii. We want him to be filled with excitement about that and want to gain his strength. If we had to leave tomorrow, we would cancel. A lot has to happen in one week. I don't hear the excitement about going in his voice or see it on his face.

Please pray for Jay and I to get the rest we need to care for Trey and to be able to comprehend the roller coaster instructions we are given at St Jude. Nothing is ever clear cut. When there are so many hands in the pot calling the shots, it's hard to know which instructions to follow. I am fighting a headache. Honestly, I have done well with my migraines not bothering me. God is good!

I know what Trey means when he says he gains strength from cards and letters. I received a precious letter from one of our church college students. It touched my heart as she always has. Her father was one of Trey's first basketball coaches when he was in kindergarten. Carlye Williams, I love you and you brought joy to this heart! It just proves, like Chip, her father, when investing in children's lives it pays great returns. Invest in children! Meanwhile, I carry Carlye's letter in my wallet. #prayfortrey

This scripture was given to me by another one of our precious youth whom I love, Jessica Faulk. Thank you for ministering to me!

"As for God, his way is perfect: the Lord's word is flawless; He shields all who take refuge in him. For who is God besides the Lord? And who is the Rock except our God? It is God who arms me with

strength and keeps my way secure. He makes my feet like the feet of a deer; He causes me to stand on the heights. He trains my hands for battle; my arms can bend a bow of bronze. You make your saving help my shield, and your right hand sustains me; your help has made me great."
Psalm 18:30-35

April 29, 2012

We should be going home soon. Except for a few bites, Trey has not eaten in a couple of days. He is also not drinking except to take medications. A respiratory therapist has been coming in every couple of hour exercising his lungs. My biggest fear is that pneumonia will set in very quickly. His main complaint is still his nausea. Every drug he takes for nausea makes him sleepy. Periodically, he wakes up and asks what day it is. When we tell him, he does not believe it because he has slept through entire days. How can he gain any strength when he is sleeping through entire days? The room is kept dark and the visitors are few. When they are here, they remain quiet so Trey can rest.

He is frustrated about taking more pills. That's been his frustration from the beginning! He doesn't want to take 30 pills and says he would rather stay in the hospital. Once, in desperation, he commented, "I thought hospitals were supposed to make you feel better."

We have worked on all the medications he needs to take with us to Hawaii, which was a battle. We want him to enjoy the trip as much as possible. For one week only, there will be no TPN. Our doctors and Karen Williams supported us in that decision but it was not unanimous with everyone at the hospital. Jay will infuse fluids each night and they will run all night long. It will be just enough sugar to give him some energy the next day, along with his medications.

We are all battling frustration at this point. So, I insisted it was time for him to go home. Maybe being at home will make him feel a little better. He will come back to St. Jude tomorrow to see his oncologist in the clinic. Hopefully, he will not sleep through it! Please pray for all his medications to fall into place and the nausea to go away!

CHAPTER 15

WHAT ARE YOUR GOALS?

"But the goal of our instruction is love from a pure heart and a good conscience and a sincere faith."
1 Timothy 1:5

April 30, 2012

Today I received the following email, "I have a very important question that may seem offensive but it is NOT meant to be at all. You speak often about improving Trey's quality of life. You also spoke about not being about to be healed from his type of cancer except if a miracle occurs (hopefully). Because of this I was wondering WHY Trey has to do school work if he is most likely going to die anyway. I don't mean to be rude I am just curious. If I were dying the LAST thing I would want is to do my school work. Thanks, I definitely hope he gets better."

Our family believes very much that GOD, not man, sets the parameters of death. Man gives us numbers based upon statistics. God formed Trey in my womb and God will decide the day and the hour he will be taken home. We don't know when that will be. I am not saying we don't listen to the doctors, because we do!

In the meantime, in order for someone who is ill to maintain their faith in God, their strength and belief in what THEY can do, they must have goals. Finishing 10th grade is a goal for Trey. Today, after throwing up much of last night, he is going to spring practice for football to be fitted for equipment for the fall. The doctor at West Clinic said it was his goal to have him back on the field in the fall. Without goals, we would all be spinning in circles. Trey is a goal-oriented person. Jay and I taught him to be that way;

to seek out the purpose God has for his life. We believe it's important to strive to be something and to give back. Jay and I were so touched when the coaches wanted to set up a tent for Trey to sit under today while he watched practice. But, Trey wanted to walk out on the field, like all his other teammates, and watch. It is a very hot day and Trey's energy didn't last long. The team was stoked to see him on the field. I was not able to go, but when he got home, he was jabbering about how the line should have done this and the receivers should have run this route. If anything, it gave his mind energy and determination.

He has other goals - going to college, buying a car and goals for his schedule for next school year. If Trey didn't have these goals, he would give up. Trey is NOT about giving up. He is about PERSEVERING! It's his character. It develops and deepens his faith and trust in the Lord. Trey has never been the leader of the pack, but we have always made him feel like he was in value. He has always been a silent leader. I want others to understand Trey's faith, hopefully, they will gain the same goal-oriented characteristics of Trey. Push on toward the goal and never stop fighting!

One day, Trey will be able to say to the Lord as it says in 2 Timothy 4:7:

"I have fought the good fight, I have finished the race, I have kept the faith."

He is still fighting the fight. With many prayers, he will finish this race on earth by keeping the faith. If not, he will be, as Trey says, healthy in heaven. We are not about giving death victory. Not yet!

May 1, 2012

Please take time to pray for Trey today. I don't say that lightly. I never ask for prayer for Trey without a heavy heart.

He is very sick and we cannot pinpoint why he is throwing up, a recurrent theme in this journey. He has been throwing up since Sunday night and is now running a fever. Fever is always a bad warning sign. We are in constant contact with St. Jude while waiting for the home health nurse to come assess him. We will go from there.

Neither Jay nor Trey will want this posted, but people need to know how serious this is today. Trey is now down to 113 pounds and needs to eat. We beg God to give him strength and the ability to eat, enjoy it, and NOT have diarrhea! That would be a dream!

Hawaii is also his dream. We are praying that dream still comes true. Please pray with us that God will give the doctors wisdom to know what the answer is for Trey today, Trey will bounce back, and we will be ready to party with friends on Thursday and head to Hawaii on Sunday. God please hear our prayers!

Jesus Calling - May 1

> *You are on the path of My choosing. There is no randomness about your life. Here and Now comprise the coordinates of your daily life. Most people let their moments slip through their fingers, half-lived. They avoid the present by worrying about the future or longing for a better time and place. They forget that they are creatures who are subject to the limitations of time and space. They forget their Creator, who walks with them only*

in the present. Every moment is alive with My glorious Presence, to those whose hearts are intimately connected with Mine. As you give yourself more and more to a life of constant communion with Me, you will find that you simply have no time for worry. Thus, you are freed to let My Spirit direct your steps, enabling you to walk along the path of Peace.

"And which of you by worrying can add a single hour to his life's span? If then you cannot do even a very little thing, why do you worry about other matters?" Luke 12:25-26

#prayfortrey

May 2, 2012

Mom and Dad are weary and so is Trey! But things are getting better. All I have to do is give a shout out on Twitter and Facebook and my prayer warriors start praying. It is such a blessing to watch God at work and see Trey go from throwing up one day and not able to get out of bed to. . .wait for it. . .going to spring football practice today at Collierville High School! Yes, he did. Imagine that, football being a motivator. He was only able to sit and watch, but it was a major accomplishment for him to get out of the bed and make it to the field. That has been his GOAL all week! We are so proud of him! Again, never think your prayers are too small for God.

His next goal is tomorrow. He must conquer the dreaded EOCs. These are the tests given by the Shelby County Schools to high school students. Thank you, Ms. Krotzer for volunteering to administer the tests at our house tomorrow. Say a prayer for Trey as he starts at 8:30 a.m. It will be a long day for him. He had the option to put these off until July, for medical reasons, but HE SAID NO. Yes, proud again.

Our pastor came to visit yesterday although Trey might have slept through part of it. At some point, I stuck my head in and Trey's phone rang.

"This is who?", Trey asked, "Who?"

Pastor Charles and I looked at each other and just shrugged our shoulders. It sounded like someone had dialed the wrong number.

"Tim Tebow?!" Trey said

I don't who was smiling bigger - me, Charles or Trey. I immediately ran to get Jay. Actually, I was screaming. All I could hear was Trey's side of the conversation until he let me listen to a little bit through his phone. They talked about Trey's favorite scripture, James 1:2-3. They also talked about football, what position he played, what school he went to, etc. It was nice to hear Tim talk about the Lord to Trey.

After they chatted, I heard Tim say "Can I pray for you?"

"Sure," answered Trey.

What a blessing! Trey immediately tweeted, *"Yep Tim Tebow just called me. Amazing guy, I am so thankful and blessed. #amazed #glorytoGod."*

There are two events on Saturday, May 5. There is the Fair on the Square in Collierville where Tailgate for the Cure will have a booth. They are the organization that is supporting Trey. Please visit the booth if you come to the Fair. Also, there is a three on three basketball tournament at Ridgeway Baptist Church for Trey's benefit. We hope to visit both events. I'm not sure if Trey will be able to make it, but I will try to be there. When Trey can't attend, Jay usually stays home and I am the public face for the family.

Reality is setting in; we fly out Sunday morning for Hawaii! He is finally getting so excited and we are too. Why Hawaii? Several years ago, Jay and I took a cruise of the Hawaiian Islands. When we came home, it is all we talked about. Trey wasn't happy when we didn't take him and Collin! Trey loves to travel as much as we do. Tomorrow night, we'll find out more about the details of the trip at the reveal party and we're SO excited. So many people have made this dream come true and there is no way to thank them all. I will be posting pictures while we're gone but I have to get us all packed first. We fly out at 6 a.m. Sunday morning!

Mom and Dad are still tired. It has been very hard to work, even just until 3, come home to wash clothes, get things done around the house, return calls, dinner, and whatever else needs attention. I'm just being honest!

Jay tried to rest today, but I called twice and interrupted him. I wish I could have let him rest. This is so mentally taxing. Trey is still having problems sleeping, so he has his share of mid-day naps. My Family Medical Leave begins on May 8, while we are in Hawaii. So, when we return, I will officially be on leave. I will work on a limited basis, to keep the schedule flowing and but my hours will be flexible. We'll see how that works out.

Since we are preparing to leave for Hawaii, we have a protocol set for our trip with his medications. Karen Williams was so wonderful to put everything on paper for us.

His medication regimen will be as follows:
Scheduled Daily:
    Kytril Patch for nausea
    Scopolamine Patch for nausea
    Dexamethasone 4 mg bid (Steriod)
    Pancrelipase 5 capsules with meals, 2 with snacks

Zantac 150 mg twice daily

Prilosec 40 mg daily

Phenergan 25 mg at bedtime

Travel Days:

Pain:

Oxycodone 5 mg: 1-2 tabs as needed for pain every 4-6 hours

Nausea:

Phenergan 25 mg tablet before boarding plane

Lorazepam 1-2 mg (Ativan)

Kytril Patch

During Vacation

Pain: Oxycodone 5 mg: 1-2 tabs as needed for pain every 4-6 hours

Nausea:

Kytril Patch

Phenergan 12.5-25 mg (1/2 tab-1 tab) as needed for nausea—try ½ tab first

(gel will sweat off in heat)

Lorazepam 1-2 mg every 6 hours as needed for nausea

Compazine Suppository only if nausea resistant

Hydration at night: 2L/8 hours (pump should program rate)

Fatigue: Ritalin 15 mg in morning after breakfast and again mid-day

Sleep habits: don't stay up/out late. Try to maintain routine of bed around 10:00 p.m., mid-day nap, with gentle activity during day as tolerated. Remember, steroids can cause muscle wasting. Walking around some is good, if tolerable. Watch heat)

Diarrhea: Imodium at onset of "rumbling" stomach or with first diarrhea episode

Insomnia: Amitriptyline 50 mg at bedtime, Sleep habits

As I was picking up some of these medications before our trip, I ran into Dr. Sara. I told her my main concern is Trey's appetite and nausea while we are on our trip. She mentioned a drug, Marinol, she uses for some of her patients struggling to gain weight. Her concern was how some patients react to it. We decided it was best to wait until after we return from Hawaii to start this new medication. I am ready for any medication to increase his appetite!

Our prayer request for Trey is that he will start and continue to eat. Tonight, he ate a bowl of chicken and rice, his first meal in 6 days. I encouraged him not to be afraid to eat. He needs to eat to gain strength because we will not be taking the TPN to Hawaii. We just want him to be able to eat and not have bad stomach cramps. That's a lot to ask.

He had enough strength to go to spring football practice today. It is amazing what motivates him. But maybe that is the motivation he needs.

He tweeted, *"Man I'm too excited to see my boys at spring practice...Wish I could be out there with ya'll #timetotakeover."*

My friend, Hollee Lott, shared this with me tonight and it touched my heart.

"We wait in hope for the Lord; he is our help and
our shield. In him our hearts rejoice, for we trust
in his holy name. May your unfailing love be with
us, Lord, even as we put our hope in you."
Psalms 33:20-22

We have told Trey and Collin for a week to work on packing for the trip. Some people just throw in a pair of swim trunks and a couple of t-shirts and they are ready for the beach. Those people have never travelled with Trey Erwin! Donna, Julianne and I sat on the floor, today, and watched Trey pick out every color of Polo to match all his shorts, pants, swim trunks, and Nike Elite socks. We had to convince him he didn't need to take five pairs of shoes. I am praying he has enough energy to wear all the clothes he is laying out to pack.

The packing and arguing about what he didn't need wore us all out for the day. But, there was still a party to attend. We had the reveal party at the home of Kevin and Melissa McEniry. Melissa worked so hard to coordinate all of the arrangements. He had been receiving gifts, hints for the reveal party, every couple of days leading up to this week. He knew he was going to Hawaii, but didn't know where he was staying or any of the details. Almost daily, he would receive something - a Polo bathing suit, a pair of Rayban's, Polo t-shirts. It was like Christmas when the UPS man showed up. Normally, medication was being delivered when FedEx or UPS would come so gifts were a nice change of pace.

Before we left for the reveal party, I found Trey in his room, crying. He was sitting in his recliner, just crying. I immediately went to my knees and asked him what was wrong. Jay heard Trey crying and came upstairs. Trey, exhausted, and he was worried about us. I told him he had no reason to be worried about us; we would be fine. He was also worried about Collin.

At this point, the disease is getting the best of him. He just kept telling me he wanted to be normal. I thought it was time for me to get tough and help him face some facts. I was very firm with him as my heart was breaking.

"Trey," I said, "you are fighting the battle of your life. If you are not mentally fit, the enemy will sneak in when you are weak. The battle will get even harder down the road and you need to be strong."

"I just don't understand what is happening to me," he said.

I fully believe Satan was trying to attack Trey while he was weak. He had not been able to eat. Now, both eating and not eating were causing nausea. It was one of very few breakdowns Trey has ever had. He didn't question his disease or his situation. After our talk, we prayed, he felt better and was ready to get into the shower. I came downstairs and found Jay and his mother in tears. The reality of the cancer was beginning to get to all of us.

When it was time to leave for the party, Trey could not get out of the house. This was typical for most of our important outings. We were running late. His stomach was cramping and he was incredibly weak and pale. I hoped, when we got to the McEniry's house and Trey saw all his friends, he would perk up. It didn't work. It took him five to ten minutes to get out of the car. When people began to surround the car, I opened the door and explained he was not feeling well. Then, Trey got out of the car. I think the welcome reception overwhelmed him and he didn't know how to handle it.

Everything was decorated with the Hawaiian theme, right down to the cake shaped like a surfboard. There were hula dancers, photographers, and sponsors of Trey's Wish, many people we had never met. We got all our information on the Sheraton Hotel, the same place Jay and I stayed when we cruised the islands. After many photographs and tasty food, Trey could not stand much more.

The cancer has definite affected is his sensory processing. He is very sensitive to light and sounds. I think drugs are causing this problem more than the cancer. He begged to leave and I could not hold him off any longer.

We said our goodbyes. It was a wonderful night sponsored by the Make a Wish Foundation.

The next morning, I apologized for my "tough love" speech by sending Trey a text:

TREY: I couldn't eat breakfast, even the toaster strudel.

LISA: "Do you know why? Are you nauseated? Cramps?"

TREY: "I think the Ritalin is taking my appetite away."

I checked on it and asked him how many he takes. He told me three! I talked to the nurse practitioner at St. Jude and she was working on the protocol for us to take to Hawaii. I reminded Trey of the talk we had earlier about nausea and pregnant women. I had to remind him nausea is part of this disease, but it does not necessarily mean he will throw up each time. I asked Trey to make it his goal to start drinking anything he feels like, even if it is Monsters!

LISA: "I love you and you can do this! "With man nothing is possible, but with God, all things are possible." Matt. 19:26"

Sometimes all the "I love you's" don't help.

TREY: "Ok that still doesn't answer why it feels weird to eat and why it is happening now all of a sudden."

I went back to what the doctors had told us. There would come a time when he will totally lose his appetite. Then, he would have to make the choice to eat, whether or not he was hungry. I told him this was a mental decision, just like so many others he has to make for himself. Then, I mentioned the doctors were considering an appetite stimulant.

"More pills," he said.

Yes, I thought to myself. If that's what it takes, more pills it is.

Since the pregnancy analogy obviously didn't work, I texted him another:

LISA: "Diabetics deal with it every day of their lives. I am not going to let you give up."

TREY: "Give up? I am just wondering why it's happening."

Finally, the words I want to hear. I'm proud he wants to know what happening with his body. At the same time, I don't have the answers he wants to hear. And some of them might not be the right answers. Sometimes it is hard to explain the unexplainable to the one you love the most.

LISA: "When you have a question, you need to text Karen. I told you why because I asked her exactly what you said. I wanted to know too. It's okay to ask, but be ready for a medical answer and a medical fix."

Saturday was a busy day for us with Fair on the Square, packing, and other activities. Trey was at home texting me constantly:

TREY: "Mom, I ate cinnamon toast crunch and it was good!"

TREY: "Mom, I ate gummy bears from Ms. Melissa and they were yummy!"

He could have eaten dog food and I would have been happy. But he was happy. And his attitude and outlook had changed.

CHAPTER 16

HAWAII! WE ARE ON OUR WAY!

"Delight yourself in the Lord, and He will give you
the desires of your heart."
Psalms 37:4

May 6, 2012

In the wee hours of the morning, a limo arrives, courtesy of Joe and Lee Duncan, to take us to the airport. Our flight is scheduled to leave at 6 a.m. We arranged to have a wheelchair for Trey at every airport stop. Thankfully, he didn't argue.

We are on our way with a little delay. Our flight out of Memphis left over an hour late, so guess what? We missed our connecting flight out of Atlanta. There are no other flights on any other airlines until tomorrow morning. They booked us before we got off the plane.

I found an airline employee and started explaining that my son was a St. Jude cancer patient, ALL his medications were on a plane on their way to Hawaii and this was unacceptable. They didn't seem to care! I cannot imagine!

There was a couple at the counter next to me on their way out of the country. If they missed their flight, they would have to pay for their entire honeymoon package and without making it to their destination. The poor bride was crying. As we all went to sit in the seats in the waiting area, the groom told me how to tweet the customer representative for the airline. We exchanged names and he asked if we were from Collierville, Tennessee.

"Yes," I said, "why?"

"I recognize your name," he said. "Is that your son?", he asked, pointing toward Trey.

They knew Trey. My heart immediately went out to them. Eventually, they were able to get on a flight and meet their honeymoon destination.

We fly out of Atlanta tonight at 7 pm. We are hanging out in the airport until then. Trey does not have the energy to move around the airport and we don't need for him to use up what energy he has. We will be flying to Los Angeles, arriving around 9:30 p.m. We will spend the night in a hotel and fly out around 8:30 in the morning for Hawaii. That will push our arrival in Hawaii a day later. I am working on getting the hotel to allow us to stay an extra day, either on Make a Wish or us. We will probably be paying for it but it will be worth it. This is the trip of a lifetime and I will not let an airline take it away from Trey or Collin.

Maybe the delay was for the sole purpose of meeting Scott Hamilton! I am not shy. When he walked by, I ran to catch him and talk to him. I explained who I was and told him about Trey.

"Where is he?", he asked. "I'd like to meet him."

Just returning from his own check-up in Cleveland, he was so encouraging to Trey. I was vibrating as I stood there listening to him. He beat cancer, not once, but twice. I guess there is a reason today's verse is James1:2-3, Trey's favorite.

"Consider it pure joy, my brethren, when encountering various trials, knowing that the testing of your faith produces endurance."

Trey is handling the layover in Atlanta very well but it's not as easy for the rest of us. Just pray this continues for Trey since his fluids are on a plane somewhere on their way to Hawaii. It will be a long day.

Trey tweeted, *"In Atlanta and we are flying to LA at 7 tonight staying at a hotel and then flying to Hawaii tomorrow #planschangefast #makingthemostofit"*

May 8, 2012

After seven hours in the Atlanta airport, we finally left for Los Angeles at 7:10 p.m. and arrived in Los Angeles around 9:30 p.m. It was actually a 4 1/2 to 5 hour flight because of the time change. With Trey's condition, I cannot imagine flying in coach. They took care of him in first class and he actually slept some. We all have our headphones to watch movies. Thankfully, he drifted off to sleep with his headphones on.

Delta put us up at the Westin hotel, without luggage or Trey's fluids. Luckily, we had some of his most important medications with us. They gave us meal vouchers, but we ate on the plane and were exhausted. We got to the hotel and collapsed.

Monday morning, Trey didn't wake up feeling well. So, I called out to my prayer warriors. It took everything he had to take his morning medications and shuffle out the door. Unlike the hospital, there wasn't a wheelchair at every corner! We kept telling him we could not miss the shuttle to the airport for our 8:45 a.m. flight.

We already had boarding passes so all we had to do is go through TSA. In Los Angeles, they stopped me with my big bag of drugs. I was the first to go through. I pointed to Trey and told them my son has cancer. We were wearing our Make a Wish t-shirts and, when I looked at the TSA officer, I know my face said, "Really?" It might have said a little more than that.

We finally got on the plane to Hawaii. I was sitting by Trey and I got out Jesus Calling to read for the morning. We read it together because Trey was a bit queasy. This is the last paragraph for May 7:

> Do not fear what this day, or any day, may
> bring your way. Concentrate on trusting Me

*and on doing what needs to be done. Relax
in My sovereignty remembering that I go
before you, as well as with you, into each
day. Fear no evil, for I can bring good out of
every situation you will ever encounter.*

Trey and I just looked at each other and smiled.
"Mom, you want to watch a movie?" he asked.
"You go ahead," I said, "but try to rest."
Jay and Collin were seated next to us. I think the
excitement was growing. We would land in Hawaii.

May 8, 2012

As we got closer and closer, Trey started getting more
and more chatty. He and Collin were getting so excited,
which was contagious for Jay and me. I am so glad I got to
sit by him on that leg of the flight, even though we didn't
see anything coming into Hawaii. I told Trey that was okay
because he would see it all from his helicopter flight.

We landed in Hawaii with a lei greeting, got our bags and
rental car. Also greeting us was the Vogt family, Jack, Mary
and their four children! Jack is a captain in the U.S Coast
Guard and he'll be flying the guys in the helicopter. Mary
set up surf lessons and our photography session. God
definitely reaches across the country to bring people
together.

Mary's brother lives in Collierville and has been following
Trey's story. When he found out we were going to Hawaii,
he had Mary contact our church to offer the flight and surf
lessons. It took me a while to contact Mary, but, once I did,
I was blessed. Her oldest daughter Joanna, goes to
Auburn, and Hannah, John, and Sam are homeschooled.
John is Trey's age and Sam is Collin's age. They have just
taken us in while we are here in Hawaii.

When we got in the rental car and began to drive, Trey went into shock at the beauty and awesomeness of Hawaii. He said people were texting him asking him if it was better than Florida. He just laughed and said it beats Florida by miles! The drive from the airport to the hotel is not like driving the coastline of the beaches in Panama City because the water isn't visible very often. The boys were very anxious to see water amidst the tall buildings and shipyards.

Since Jay and I had been before, I knew when we were getting close to the hotel. I was able to tease the boys about things to come and what to look for, like the Ralph Lauren store. As soon as I saw the Hilton Hawaiian Hotel, I knew we were close to the Sheraton. When we arrived the boys entered the lobby, they were starstruck. I just told them to keep walking straight through the lobby. They wanted to stop at each shop on each side of them - candy stores, ice cream shops, t-shirt shops. Eventually, they reached open air and the infinity pool looking straight into the ocean. To the left, they saw a big mountain and a long stretch of beach. They sat, vibrating, while I got our room keys.

The elevator buttons are in the middle of the room, not next to the elevators. There are plenty of elevators. The elevator took us up to the 30th floor; the hotel only has 31! We kept walking around the hall looking for room 3036 and came upon huge, double wooden doors. They were the kind of doors that always make you wonder what is on the other side. Trey and Collin said they looked like something from the Narnia movies. Well, those were the doors marked 3036! We walked in and just stopped. We were in the Leahi suite. I laughed to myself because I had asked about our view at the front desk. There were three balconies and we could see EVERYTHING! Trey and Collin have the view of Diamondhead.

I went to join Trey on his balcony as he was taking pictures. His Twitter picture, Waikiki Beach and Diamondhead in the background, just said "Woww." His first tweet from Hawaii said, *"Just arrived in paradise."*

While Trey was soaking in the scenery, Collin wanted to get to the pools as soon as possible. We began to get our clothes unpacked and I realized I didn't have the Make a Wish debit card with all the money. I forgot it at the house so my sister is sending it by FedEx. I hope to get it today. What organized brain I ever had is just about gone!

Everyone was hungry, even Trey. Before we went to eat, we had a family meeting. Make a Wish had two excursions planned for us, surf lessons and snorkeling, both requiring a 20 minute boat ride. Because of Trey's trouble with nausea and knowing we would be able to do these activities with the Vogt family, we decided to cancel them. I didn't want to chance him getting sick on a scheduled tour and not being able to return to land or the hotel.

On the way to the Cheesecake Factory, Trey said, "Man, I feel so good. I don't even feel like I have cancer!" I wanted to cry. Jay and I told him to just keep feeling that way. He ate a whole burger at the Cheesecake Factory and ordered key lime cheesecake to go. It was the most he had eaten in weeks!

We walked a little, went to the ABC store (their Walgreens) and I kept waiting for him to tell us he needed to go to the bathroom.

"What are we going to do now?" was all he said.

What else do you do in Hawaii but head to the pool? It was about 6 p.m. and the pool starts closing at dusk. We stayed in the hot tub for as long as we could. With Trey being so thin, the hot tub felt so good to him, but I was afraid he would not realize he was being burned by the water.

Then, it was time to take in some shopping! Before we went shopping, Trey got up and fell flat on his face. He got rug burns on his wrists and hands. Collin cracked up; Jay laughed a little and said, "You alright, son?"

I didn't laugh because he's been a fall risk before. It happened so fast, we could not catch him. It reminds me of his weakness and the last thing we need is an infection due to rug burns. His skin is so thin, the carpet took it off.

We got Trey a new bathing suit since his other bathing suit falls off. We picked up some things for Collin and decided to call it a night. It didn't take long before we all hit the bed. Welcome to Hawaii!

May 8, 2012

Trey woke up this morning with a fever. He did a lot yesterday so it's no surprise his body is paying for it. It is 1:30 p.m. in Hawaii and he has been on fluids since around 11 a.m. He is sleeping. He wanted to sleep like on a normal vacation and meet us at the pool around 1 p.m. I reminded him this is NOT a normal vacation and he is NOT normal. I hated reminding him of that, but he has to take care of himself. Trey ended up on fluids all day. I think the flight coupled with the time change just really knocked him down.

After he received the fluids, he felt so much better. It is remarkable what fluids can do for your body. I took Collin to the beach where he quickly realized the Hawaiian beach is much different than a Florida beach. And, the water is not as warm. We spent most of our day at the pool. The pool was a little chilly for most of the adults, so we all gathered in the hot tubs! Jay didn't leave Trey while he was sleeping, just in case.

Since Trey had been in bed most of the day, he woke up a little hungry. Jay and I decided to take the boys to Duke's, a cool restaurant on the beach known for their hamburgers and such. We all loved Duke's so much we all left with tanks, t-shirts, and sweat-shirts.

Trey is starting to get back to his routine. We are blessed to be staying on the floor of the Leahi Club. Our room was on the concierge level, so we were given access to the Leahi Club that serves breakfast and hors d'oeurves in the late afternoon. We have discovered their oatmeal, bagels, and most of all, the fruit. Trey wakes early in the morning because he cannot sleep. I often wake to find a 5 foot 7 inch teen standing over me at 6 a.m. ready for breakfast!

"Come on mom, go eat oatmeal with me," he says.

During those early morning breakfasts, Trey and I would talk about what we would that day and what he wanted to accomplish.

"Mom, look!", Trey shouted one morning. Cascading over the tall building into the water was a double rainbow. He immediately got his phone out and took a picture. We captured quite a special moment in time!

We had plans to meet the Vogt family on Wednesday for surfing, paddle boarding, snorkeling, etc. Driving in Hawaii is challenging. The street names are mostly numbers, like 5A, H-2, etc. What happened to common street names? I think we would have to live here for a year, memorize routes and just forget names of streets and highways. Meeting the Vogt's in a parking lot was a good idea.

Trey has not totally regained his strength and was experiencing major stomach pain. But that didn't stop Collin. We went to a local spot where the Vogts enjoy paddle boarding and surfing. Collin picked it up like he had been doing it for months! Jay and I didn't dare attempt paddle boarding or surfing! Jay did kayak. It was very difficult to get Trey out of the van. He walked a couple of steps to where the beach and water met and got back into the van. We decided to walk across the street to get a sno cone. In Hawaii, it is their famous Hawaiian shaved ice. Trey did make it out of the van for the Hawaiian ice, but he was weak.

The evening was spent with friends, Monica and Rick Farrall and the Vogt family. Once we arrived at the Farrall home, Trey could not get out of the van. His cramps were so bad, he could not move. We had given him all his medications and I was incredibly frustrated. I don't know if I was more frustrated with Trey or his attitude! We finally convinced Trey to try to walk from the van to the house where he could lay down.

We were welcomed with open arms into an amazing home. It overlooks the ocean with a plush backyard and a beach where we found 14 turtles. I am talking turtles like you see on television! Collin and I braved crawling down the mountain of lava rocks to the small part of beach where the turtles were gathering. I told Jay and he had to get Trey down here, even if he had to carry him. Trey's pain medication had finally begun to work and he said he could walk down himself. I watched as he took each step over and between each rock just like I was watching him take his first steps. I knew I would not be able to get to him in time to catch him if he fell. Jay was much closer. There was a slip; he caught himself, and I caught my breath. He finally made it to the beach, where we were all face to face with the largest turtles we had ever seen. As the waves began to roll in over the turtles, they moved further and further up the beach.

We cooked out, watched the sunset, threw a little football, and the adults had a nice time relaxing as we listened to the kids laugh. Jay and I had wanted to take the kids to a luau while we were in Hawaii, but I would not trade anything for the view from the backyard of the Farrall home where Trey and Collin watched the big burning sun set over the ocean. What a wonderful evening we will never forget.

The Hawaiian food was attacking Trey's digestive system in an extreme manner. Trey spent most of each the morning in the bathroom. We had to send Trey's pajamas to the laundry every morning. They were returned in our suite later in the evening. When the sun came up over Diamondhead on Thursday, we were ready to FLY! We met Jack at the Coast Guard base where he had arranged for three of us to be taken around the island in a Coast Guard helicopter. Trey, Collin and I went with two other Coast Guard pilots. It was amazing to fly with the door open watching Trey snapping pictures with his phone. He had no fear as he leaned out the edge of the helicopter.

The Coast Guard treated us first class. They gave Trey his flight suit, made him Admiral for the day and gave him a rescue diver's fin with his name on it. We all received flight suit badges with our name on it, t-shirts, lunch. As we were pulling out of the parking lot of the hanger, I felt the van roll over something. I looked in the back seat and didn't see the movie camera. Yes, the movie camera was on the back of the van and now in small pieces.

From there, we went on to surfing lessons! When we arrived on the beach to surf, I knew I would not be surfing. Jay and one of the surfers from Access Surf walked Trey to the water after they had learned how to bend, lean, and stand on their board. As soon as Trey got to the edge of the water, he didn't have the strength to stand. When the small waves hit his legs, it would have knocked him down if Jay had not been there to hold him up. He said it was okay if he didn't surf and he came to sit with me. My heart just broke at that moment for Trey. He began to shiver and get anxious. The sun was so bright, he had to keep his sunglasses on most of the time because of medications making him sensitive to light. Jay and Collin attempted surfing. Let's just say Collin was very successful and took to it right away. I had a blast watching Collin conquering something he set his mind to doing. Trey was so proud of Collin. Access Surf is a great organization!

I am very thankful I was able to receive emails while I in Hawaii. On Thursday, I received an email from Kyle Munyon, the person responsible for taping Trey's testimony. I viewed it for the first time and could not get it out of my mind. Here I am, in beautiful Hawaii listening to Trey tell of his battle with cancer, the sound of the Grizzlies announcer in the background of his video, and the emphasis of prayer did come across. It was like on a reel to reel in my head, playing over and over.

Because of Trey's lack of strength, we didn't get far off the beaten path. We ate at the Cheesecake Factory twice, Duke's twice, and Margueritaville. Some of those times were for lunch. We were lucky to have a pizza place, and a Baskin Robbins in our hotel. Trey's energy appeared in the evening, so, every night, we shopped till he dropped. We learned every inch of Ralph Lauren and the Foot Locker, where he bought a different pair of Nike Elite socks every time we went into the store. One of the retail workers started to recognize Trey every time he came into the store and it became a running joke with the Nike Elite socks. One thing Trey did enjoy in Hawaii was the shopping.

Friday morning, I began arranging with the hotel and the airlines for the day we missed due to our flight mishap leaving Memphis. I explained our situation to the manager of the hotel. They were gracious to allow us another night in Hawaii. So, we don't fly out until Monday.

When I explained what kind of trip we were on, the airline also waived our fee for changing our flight. Friday afternoon, we all went to the infinity pool. This was the first time for Trey to get in the water. It was a little cold for Trey, but I am glad he finally felt like getting in and he can say he did it. He got a little sun and he needed it. Some of the morning, Jay, Trey and I spent at the pool while Collin enjoyed the pool slides. The Hawaiian breeze can hit you just right and keep you warm until you have fallen asleep in the poolside chairs.

The Vogt family was very gracious to arrange for us to meet on Friday at the Admiral's house, where there is a lighthouse out on a point on Diamondhead for family pictures. It is absolutely breathtaking. Trey knew how important the pictures were to me and I believe they were important to him too. It is not every day you stand at the top of a lighthouse in Hawaii looking out into the deep blue Pacific Ocean. It is a working lighthouse and it was very warm at the top. Getting us all out of the lighthouse was quite comical!

The gardens at the Admiral's home made for a spectacular backdrop for our pastel shirts, white pants and shorts. There seemed to be a hibiscus of every color and flowers I would never be able to describe. We took our shoes off and walked on the soft cool Bermuda grass that was like bright green carpet. Our pictures will be magnificent.

We decided to make Saturday a day of rest all of us. We didn't go to the pool or beach. Trey had enough sun the day before and, sometimes, when you are on vacation, you just need to have a rest day. Resting didn't keep us from shopping that evening, though. Trey and I shopped just about every night! MY SON LOVES TO SHOP! He will make a wife very happy one day, just like his father!

Sunday was a special Mother's Day. My children bought me Pandora charms for my bracelet. Trey bought me a turtle and Collin bought me a dolphin. Sunday morning, I woke up and Trey had an envelope next to my bed with a handwritten note that said, "I love you thisssss much". With the envelope was a picture of the two of us in Knoxville at the University of Tennessee spring game. It is one of the most special gifts I have ever received.

Trey had really started to feel better the last couple of days. Sunday was the day of the 7th game of the Grizzlies playoff series. We invited John, Mary and Jack's son, to come watch the game with us in our suite. It was strange getting up and watching a basketball game at 7 a.m. because of the six hour time difference, but we wanted to watch our Grizzlies in Hawaii. Later in the day, the Vogt family game by for Mother's Day lunch while Collin, Sam, and Joanna went surfing. From 30 stories up, we had to make sure which dot we were watching surf! We had fun taking pictures on the balcony and being goofy. As the day came to a close, we knew this would be the last time we would see the Vogt family in Hawaii. They will soon be transferring to Alaska with the Coast Guard.

It is amazing how God can bring two Christian families together with so many things in common. He blessed us so much through this family. We will never forget everything they did for us during our trip, so unselfishly. They were such a Christ-like example. We missed each other before we left!

On Monday, we were able to take our time to get things together before we had to be at the airport. Our room was reserved until Tuesday, at no extra charge, so we didn't have to store our luggage. We were all able to do last minute things we wanted to get done. Collin did great all week. Again, I am so thankful God brought him Sam Vogt, a friend his age with things in common and for the things he learned. Now, he and Trey both want to move to Hawaii.

The flights home were smooth and we all slept most of the way. It was much easier on Trey to fly most of the night so he could rest. We all are trying to adjust to Memphis time. Otherwise, Trey is feeling good. It is hard to conceive flying out of one city at 10 p.m. on Monday night and arriving home on Tuesday at 1:30 in the afternoon. It is exhaustion on top of a full week of unbelievable adventure!

CHAPTER 17

BACK TO REALITY

*"But as for me, I watch in hope for the Lord;
I wait for God my Savior, my God will hear me."* Micah 7:7

When we arrived home, Trey tweeted, *"Home sweet home, Miss HI like I've been living there in paradise forever but comin home and havin support and people caring beats any trip."*

We came home to such a blessing. As of today, Thursday, May 17, Trey finished school as a sophomore at Collierville High School. Thank you Lord! It was a combined effort from so many people at Collierville High School. Trey's class sponsor, Ms. Krotzer, had to read most of Trey's End of Course tests to him because of his vision. We had so many teachers volunteer to help with these tests. Trey could not have finished school without his homebound teacher, Katie Doyle. She was so patient during all the times we had to cancel at 8 a.m. because he woke up sick. Most students could not sit through class for three hours, but Trey was able to handle his treatments and sit at the kitchen bar while he struggled over English, Geometry, World History, Health Science Education, and Biology. There were many late nights of homework when he felt his strength was at its best. It was a goal Trey set out to accomplish and he did it. Trey tweeted today, *"Had a great day today and finished all my school! First day of summer tomorrow!!...and I'll be at St. Jude all day. #nothowiplannedit"*

Also, Collin is taking his books back to school. What a blessing after being gone on a trip and not being put behind. God knows who you need in your life and when you need them. I cannot tell you how much Jay and I felt blessed by our posse when we came home - Cindy Few, Hollee Lott, and Karen Stonebrook - my God-given posse. We call it "doing life together".

We were scheduled to attend the Victor Marx Story on Tuesday night at Highpoint Church, but Trey was so exhausted. We knew he would have a full day today. There was no way any of us could push ourselves without becoming physically ill. I am told the showing was a very big success. Our family is very thankful for the prayers offered before the movie by our Pastor, Charles Fowler, and the donation that was taken. You can see Trey's faith story by searching #prayfortrey at www.joshmaze.com. I pray this will lead you to think about your own faith.

"How do people make it through life without the Lord?" Trey has asked, on several occasions.

My answer to him has been simple, "Honey, I just don't know."

Tomorrow, Friday, May 18 is a big day for us. Trey has a PET scan at St. Jude. This is a big test and will tell us whether or not there has been progress with the chemotherapy. Trey has had four chemotherapy treatments and we are praying that is enough to show positive results. Please pray for progress, healing, and reduction. Trey only lost one pound while we were in Hawaii, which is wonderful! We don't know if St. Jude will put him back on the TPN or not. It makes him so sick. I know he has had some very tiring days, but putting him back on TPN just seems cruel.

May 19, 2012

Trey tweeted, *"At St. Jude today for PET scan all day...Ready to get out and go to the maroon and white game! Which one should I go for?"*

We believe we have a good report from the PET scan. It may be a little confusing comparing the first to the third, but I am going to explain as best I can. The tumor in Trey's pancreas prior to his first PET measured 4.3 x 3.2 centimeters. As of yesterday, it measured 2 x 2 centimeters. It has reduced almost half in size after four treatments. This is very good news! This is the kind of progress Dr. Tauer was hoping the treatment would produce.

Next, we are dealing with the three liver lesions. I will not lay out the dimensions, but two have been cut in half and the other two have reduced to the same size as the last PET. Again, this is good news.

Dr. Sara can look at a PET scan and then draw the explanation on a piece of paper. Without her simple explanations, we would never understand what is being told to us. Dr. Sara drew us a picture of a liver with a wedge cut out.

"This is a perfusion defect," she said "It's not uncommon. The dark circle is one of Trey's current liver lesions."

A spot did show up on the PET but all the radiologists, and Dr. Sara agreed it's not new disease. If the chemotherapy is working and reducing the current lesions, it would not make sense for a new lesion to form. We are going to keep watching it. It can be something from infection. Trey has run fever several times and that could be the cause.

The main thing we are going to be dealing with immediately are three pseudocysts next to his pancreas and stomach (one large in the front, one smaller in between, and one at the tail of the pancreas). The largest pseudocyst is as large as his original pancreatic tumor. These cysts can cause back pain, nausea, and vomiting, symptoms he has been experiencing the last two or three weeks. They are also symptoms we could not connect to anything else. These cysts occur when organs are irritated, such as the pancreas. Our main concern is the duodenum. It is showing narrowing and we don't know if this is from disease, inflammation, or obstruction of some kind. Trey does have disease in the duodenum. The doctors believe the pancreatic tumor began at the entry of where the duodenum and the pancreas meet.

Our next step is to cancel chemotherapy for Monday and see the gastroenterologist at Methodist. He will have an endoscopy which will tell us what is happening in the duodenum and pancreas. Dr. Sara said sometimes they go through the stomach and drain the cysts and let the fluid flow into the stomach. It's possible he will need a stent in his duodenum.

There's more good news. The tumor and lesions in his liver were not as bright on the PET as they were in the beginning. God is killing the cancer cells! There is a slight glow to the top of one of the cysts, the large one, which we hope is nothing. The radiologists don't think they are anything tumor related. It is all in God's hands and I trust He will take care of it.

Trey was very confused by the report. We just told him to trust that it was good. Even though we promised to tell Trey everything from the very beginning and he has been present during all of the conversations, he has slept through some of those conversations. It's understandable he might be a little confused. All of the testing and reports we received today are from St. Jude. All of these reports will be relayed this weekend to Dr. Tauer at West Clinic and we will wait for his advice. We have some other avenues in mind but want to talk to him before anything is done. We have to make sure everyone is on the same page.

Trey had a good time seeing his friends at the Collierville Maroon and White Spring Game. We are all ready for some football but, Trey has to gain a lot of weight before he can get back on the field. We keep praying each day for one pound, just one pound. It was a nice change of pace to see football friends and have Trey surrounded by them.

Instagram is relatively new to me but Trey knows all the latest technology. I noticed he posted the picture of the rainbow out the window with the caption, *"Somewhere over the rainbow, blue birds fly, and the dreams that you dream of, dreams really do come true"* "The Wizard of Oz" is one of my all-time favorite movies. The Hawaiian version of this song is what Trey downloaded on his phone because we heard it everytime the elevator doors opened in Hawaii.

I am not sure when he posted the picture because none of the family got out of bed until after 11 a.m. We did get a new drug, Marinol, to stimulate his appetite. He has not rolled out of the bed today. He is very tired. We are all very tired. I feel like half the day is gone, but I know we all need the rest.

Tonight will be a different experience in Collierville. I hope all of Memphis will show up. It is the Play for Trey Concert with Jimi Jamison and many more. Alexis Gray of American Idol will be hosting. The radio station 107.5 will be there, and there will be a presentation to Trey by Tony Allen and the Memphis Grizzlies. We are in awe of how God brings people back into our lives after years of absence. Thank you, Dr. Eric Gardner for sponsoring this event. Most of all, thank you Todd Hutchison. Without you and your entertainment company, none of this would be possible. Many Harding Academy alumni were involved with organizing this event and we are blessed to call Harding family.

For an evening in May, it was very hot. Trey was extremely tired before we left for the event. The event started at 6 p.m. and we were not able to arrive until a little after it had started. Even though I was not far away, I received a text:

TREY: "Mom, when is this over?"

LISA: "Why?"

I knew he didn't want to leave because he was not grateful or entertained. Trey was surrounded by friends, but also by people he didn't know. At times, that was uncomfortable for him. When Trey does not feel good, he gets very irritable.

TREY: "I'm hot and tired."

LISA: "We need to wait a little while."

TREY: "Ok but it's kinda weird to watch these people play because the bass player plays the organ in Sunday morn church."

We all got a laugh because it was odd to see people out of the element you normally see them. I told him the event was not to end until 10:15 p.m.

TREY: "Oh my."

As soon as the Grizzlies presented Trey with his jersey, we would need to leave. The heat was too oppressive and I didn't need him passing out. The adults enjoyed the music, probably much more than Trey, because it was music from the 80's. All he did was make fun of us. We had a good time singing and dancing in the football stands at Collierville High School and making fools of ourselves. Isn't it a parent's job to embarrass their child a few times while singing "Eye of the Tiger" at the top of your lungs?

Trey was happy too. He got to hang out with Tony Allen of the Grizzlies, receive a jersey, and get a guitar signed by Miranda Lambert who was in concert in Memphis the night before.

Our life revolves around trying to get Trey to eat. Thank you Mr. Pancreas! Our family cannot express how much the food being delivered is helping us. Yesterday, we came in from St. Jude, exhausted, and just ate cereal. It's hard to imagine how much of my mind is occupied by one thing. Bills, your house, your job, and, sometimes, your family get pushed aside. We are all-consumed and the thought of making a meal is incomprehensible. Thank you to all the families who have fed us for the last couple of months. We could not have made it without you and I cherish the sweet conversations and hugs we have when the meals are delivered.

Some days I see others living in glass houses. Their lives seem perfect with their happy little families. I honestly pray nothing like this ever happens to them. If it ever does, I hope I will be in line to take a meal and will remember what it has meant to our family.

Tonight, I am proud of Trey's tweet to his followers, *"To all my followers that don't know me personally or my story, check out http://vimeo.com/42036059 and remember all glory goes to God."*

"But I have trusted in Your lovingkindness; My heart shall rejoice in Your salvation. I will sing to the Lord, because He has dealt bountifully with me." Psalms 13:5-6

CHAPTER 18

TRANSPARENT

"Blessed is the man who trusts in the Lord,
whose confidence is in Him."
Jeremiah 17:7

May 20, 2012

My heart is heavy to share what our pastor, Dr. Charles Fowler, shared during his sermon this morning. I sent him a text and told him, I didn't know what God was doing, but I had the same feelings as I was driving to church this morning. I had the opportunity to "vent" these feelings on two separate occasions today with friends and I am thankful they listened with open hearts. They heard the same sermon I did.

Dr. Fowler preached beginning from John 10:10-15.

"The thief comes only to steal and kill and destroy; I came that they may have life, and have it abundantly."

He also talked about character. One thing I can say about Trey's character is it's transparent. Dr. Fowler's definition of character was "the person who you are when you are before God." Character is who you are when no one is looking.

As a family, we have chosen to live our faith out in the open. We don't live in a house on a hill surrounded by glass. We still live in the same house in Collierville we moved into when Collin was entering kindergarten and Trey entered third grade at Tara Oaks. We have just chosen, in the circumstance God has put us in, to put Him first in all we do to make sure we are living out His will. Just like this verse says, the thief comes to steal, but Jesus came that we may have abundant life. If there is anything we need right now, it's LIFE, abundant life.

We believe in a transformational life. We know God can take something and turn it into something good. This is evident by what God is doing in Trey's life. We have heard so many life-altering stories we pray are by God's work. We live life expectantly, even though we don't know what the next day will bring. We don't know what the next couple of hours will bring with Trey. Will he be nauseated? Throwing up? Falling down? Will he make it to the bathroom? Be awake? Asleep? Hungry? Feverish? Dehydrated? We know people have us under a microscope. Sometimes, at night, it is hard to put my head on the pillow trying to remember what I might have done to lead someone astray that day. We are just a normal family, praying for God's protection daily.

Normal is the one thing Trey would love to be. He needs encouragement from his friends and our doors are open. If he is tired, he will tell you (or we will tell you). It's summer. What normal 15 year old doesn't get excited about summer?

Dr. Fowler went on to share the following, which has been on my heart, (my paraphrase):

A person in pain often encounters two types of people...those who say "Hang in There" or those who walk, cry, and work through the pain as if it's their own. Which would you choose to have by you?

We want those willing to walk with us, cry with us, love us, hug us, knock on our door, and work this out with us. Merely, "hanging in there" is not an option! We are already hanging on to God's word. Don't be my "hang in there" friend! Sometimes, we cannot even respond to phone calls or texts, but our "walk through" friends know how much they mean to us.

So many people have asked what they could do to help. Pray! We need those prayers. We have many decisions to make regarding Trey's care, Collin's summer, calendar decisions, etc. We are mentally and emotionally drained and it is very hard to make decisions.

Dr. Fowler preached, recently, about filling the altar. It made me wonder why all of us don't have carpet burn from praying at the altar! If not for our own family, we should be praying for someone else. I told my friends today at lunch, jokingly, God gave us the altar and I am going to use it!

I am often asked "How are you doing? How is Trey doing? How is Jay? Collin?" My response is, "we are hanging in there." If I were totally transparent every time someone asked, I would take up 30 minutes of each person's time. Sometimes, I say "I am doing as well as can be expected." There are days I would love to fall apart on the spot. Since time doesn't allow, that has to be my answer.

Thankfully, God has put a strong rod in our back and, by His hand, we are held up. This morning, when the graduates walked across during the senior church service, was not one of my strong moments I so want Trey to be able to do that in a couple of years. I plead to God, each day, for his healing, strength, and future.

What about you? What kind of friend are you? What kind of friend do you want to be? Our youth mission trip is coming up and Collin will be on that trip. In order to be the hands and feet of Jesus, our youth must carry the character of Christ, including transparency, first.

After our wonderful service this morning, we were able to go to the church picnic. Trey was able to be with the family, visit with people he normally does not get to see, and see his kids from children's church. It was good to watch him with Julianne, just being goofy and enjoying life. It was a few brief moments of normal.

May 25, 2012

Julianne tweeted *"Another amazing night with Bubba :) #perfectsummer"*
Trey replied, *"@NotJusAnnieBody sure was! But you needa get some rest so you can get up early! #breakfast #gonnabeanothergoodday"*

Since Trey and his friends are out of school, he has felt so much better, especially since he has not had chemotherapy. As I was trying to figure out what the plans where for the evening, he sent me a text, "Stacia, Tim, Julianne, and Cojo are over watching "The Sandlot." How can I argue with a room full of teens watching the Sandlot?

> **Courtney Jordan's Thoughts:** The month of May 2012 was when everything became very real to me. I had to withdraw from college earlier that spring semester due to medical problems I was having; I was angry with God for that. I did not want to miss out on a semester of college, especially during my freshman year. In May, it suddenly dawned on me. If I never had to withdraw from school, I never would have gotten to spend so much quality time with Trey during his journey. It was by far one of the biggest blessings in disguise. One for which I will be forever grateful. God's timing is perfect and He is always faithful.
>
> I was hanging out with Trey and some other friends watching The Sandlot at his house.

There was some time that day when it was just Trey and me. He took advantage of this time and told me, "Cojo, I want to talk to you about my funeral." To that I responded, "Umm, Trey, I don't want to talk about your funeral. I don't want to think about that." Trey lovingly told me, "Cojo, we have to. I want my funeral to be a party, alright? I don't want people to be sad or wearing black. And I want glow sticks. Lots of glow sticks. Promise you'll make sure this is done?" We pinky swore to that.

That was the moment everything became real to me. That was the moment I was so thankful God had not only put Trey in my life, but also that he was someone I considered as my little brother and that we shared a friendship centered on Christ. That was the moment that I realized just how thankful we should be for those in our life, sick or not, because you never know the last day you can make something as little as a pinky promise with them.

We saw Dr. Ismail, the gastroenterologist with the UT Medical Group at Methodist Hospital, yesterday. He had not yet read the PET scan from last Friday at St. Jude, but agreed with Dr. Sara and Dr. Tauer. Trey will need a stent in his duodenum. When he did the ERCP when Trey was in St. Jude the first time, he predicted that would be the case. According to Dr. Ismail, the duodenum was narrow when he initially did the ERCP. At this point, we don't know if the narrowing is due to disease, an obstruction, or inflammation. We do know there is disease in the duodenum; that's new information. Dr. Ismail thinks, without looking at the scan, the tumor is growing down into the duodenum. I pray not!

The major purpose of the stent is to open the duodenum which will allow waste from the stomach and pancreas to pass more easily. This will help Trey to feel much better. It will alleviate acid reflux, some nausea, and vomiting.

The next issue discussed were the pseudocysts. We were initially told these cysts were harmless and could be drained. Dr. Ismail now says the cysts are malignant. So, draining them would cause infection, bleeding, and other problems down the road. We really don't know what to think. Again, we will wait till after the scope to decide what to do with them. I can keep telling myself God is not a God of confusion. Trust. Wait.

Trey is scheduled to have the scope next Thursday, May 31, 2012, at 1 p.m. at Methodist Hospital downtown. He may or may not spend the night. Most people go home, but we want to make sure his pain level is manageable after the procedure before taking him home.

As of today, Trey is feeling great and eating well! His color is good. He was fixing a peanut butter and jelly sandwich at midnight last night! This little break from chemotherapy has done a world of good; not only for him, but for the rest of the family. He still is having problems with his strength because some of his muscles have been destroyed. We find out next week when he will start chemotherapy again.

Before the scope and while he is feeling good, we are going to spend time together as a family, doing some things he would like to do; go to the movies and the pool. We are planning a trip to Florida the end of June and going with the church on the high school beach trip. Please pray as we plan those trips.

We have several important prayer requests. One, there will be no new disease in the duodenum; two, the cysts are not malignant; and three, the stent is easily placed.

We are so thankful for prayers. We know God hears each one. Just as He hears my prayers, he catches every tear. Sometimes the days are long, especially the nights. Sometimes, Trey texts during those times to ask medical questions:

TREY: (at 1:36 a.m. Friday morning) "Goodnight sorry that I asked you about all this stuff on short notice. I know your're tired so I'll let you sleep! Love you!"

LISA: (after answering his questions) "Love you!"

Today, I am claiming Psalms 42:8 *"The Lord will command His lovingkindness in the daytime; And His song will be with me in the night, A prayer to the God of my life."*

June 1, 2012

Trey has had a good week. It is a good week when there is no throwing up and the nausea is somewhat under control. We have had a full week and Trey has been a trooper. I texted from work:

LISA: "How are you doing?"

TREY: "Well I laid in bed till 9 and took morning medications then dad made me chocolate chip oatmeal that we saw at WalMart, the chocolate chips melted so it smelled like chocolate chips but tasted like the Hawaii oatmeal anyways then I laid back down and watched a movie and dad gave me lunch medications and the appetite pill so I ate pringles and Arizona tea then changed clothes cleaned up a little got new ringtones then Laura came over the same time Mrs. Teresa came so I showed off most off my stuff before Laura had to leave to go to work at three then Mrs. Teresa said my port looked great and she left now me and Collin are watching movies in my room and dad just left to go get Abby! And I've been texting J.D. McMillan all day talking about our siblings dating haha but yes if you haven't noticed from this text that is full of unimportant information I'm feeling great :) Did you get all of that?"

On May 29, he tweeted, *"Stay awake, stand firm in your faith, be brave, be strong. 1 Corinthians 16:13"*

Trey has been eating very well! That's, such a wonderful blessing, but he can only eat so many bowls of oatmeal. Oatmeal is his 2 a.m. meal of choice right now. Some nights he is not going to bed until midnight and he will eat then. Because of our trip to Hawaii and his scope, he has not had chemotherapy since the beginning of May. Things just needed to heal for a bit.

On Tuesday, May 29, we went to St. Jude for labs and antibiotic infusions. His white count has continued to crawl up and we don't know why. It could be because of his port or something as simple as his ingrown toenail. He should not be clipping his nails so we have made him stop because of his eyesight. Dr. Sara has now planned for a specific antibiotic infusion every month to help prevent pneumonia. He also began a ten day round of Levaquin which he has been receiving nightly.

On Wednesday, May 30, Trey woke up not feeling good. I knew what was going on. Satan knew we were giving our testimony at church. I began to text friend and told them to pray for Trey because of what was going on. I sent Trey a text and told him to look at the poster he made in his room with scripture on it and don't let Satan get to him. He called me a couple of hours later and told me he found a scripture card a friend had planted in the bathroom:

"Therefore humble yourselves under the mighty hand of God, that He may exalt you at the proper time, casting all your anxiety on Him, because He cares for you." 1 Peter 5: 6-7

What an amazing God we serve! Trey was so excited and pumped from reading His word. Satan has nothing on Our God and His word! We were able to deliver our testimony to the youth (and a lot of adults) at church without anxiety. Trey was not his normal self because of medication and proceeded to take his shirt off to show everyone his port. Otherwise, I believe God received the glory. The question and answer time was good for all of us. We are very thankful for our church giving Trey the opportunity to talk to the youth about his journey to this point. Trey tweeted after the service, *"Blessed to have @NotJus AnnieBody in my life for staying with me while I don't feel good even though she had other plans #loveyou."* We are blessed by Julianne also. She is like a daughter to us and she takes very good care of Trey and his needs.

Wednesday evening, I had a tooth start to hurt. On Thursday morning, first thing, I called my dentist and he worked me in. I ended up having a tooth pulled. While under gas, Jay texted me to tell me the doctor had called and wanted Trey at the hospital early for the scope.
LISA: "I am at the dentist under gas!"

I got a tooth pulled, picked up Julianne, and almost beat Jay and Trey to the Methodist parking lot. But, I forgot to get my own pain medication filled, big mistake!

We waited in the endoscopy lab for over two hours. Long enough for Trey to take pictures of me with his phone and call me the Phantom of the Opera with my swollen face. Trey tweeted, *"Knowing that you are in God's hands ALL the time and that he is in control relieves all emotions.*

'Bout to go into surgery!" Then he posted one of the pictures he had taken on Twitter.

They took him back at 2:30 p.m. and it took about an hour for the scope. Dr. Ismail and Dr. Fitten came out and told us the procedure was successful. They were able to place the stent where it needed to go. There is no new disease!

We were very, very confused after talking to the doctors and looking at pictures for 30 minutes. I was able to go to be with Trey in recovery so I asked Dr. Fitten to explain, in layman's terms, what occurred. He said it was the same disease, presented in a different manner causing a blockage in the duodenum. The doctors got to a point where the scope would not go any further and they knew it was blocked. After the simple explanation, we understood the pictures.

The stent will help things pass though easier. So many things connect to this duodenum - the common bile duct (from the stomach), the pancreatic duct (pancreas), the hepatic duct (liver), cystic duct (gallbladder), and much more. The best news is the entrance to the stomach was cancer free! When we saw the cancer in his duodenum and compared it to the entrance of the stomach, we understood what cancer looks like and what healthy, pink cells look like.

Dr. Ismail called today. The biopsies they took of the area in the duodenum were positive for cancer. We knew that would be the case. This is NOT new cancer. It was present when Trey was originally diagnosed on March 6. The picture of the opening of this duct is amazing. Trey was so excited when he went to the bathroom this morning and had solid poop. He had to show his mama! What can I say? He is still a boy.

I received a call today from Dr. Sara at St. Jude. They have made an appointment for us to meet with her and Dr. Tauer from West Clinic on Tuesday of next week to discuss the treatment going forward. Trey is very excited about this. Jay and I will be glad to get both doctors in one room, just like Trey. After the scope, Dr. Ismail suggested we continue the most agressive treatment. That's what he has been receiving and it has been working. He didn't recommend surgery, which is something we have been talking about. This is where our trust will totally need to be in the Lord's hands. I am sure there will be several options. But I am praying the Lord will direct the doctors to one option best for Trey.

Trey, as he said in his testimony, is frustrated when he wakes up in the morning feeling like he is not progressing physically. Some of his frustration is due to his lack of strength. Last week, he gained ONE pound for the first time since his diagnosis! That's such a praise! God is answering our prayers and we are remaining faithful to thank Him for all He has blessed us with. We are thankful for one pound because we know one can become two.

All of Trey's friends are leaving on the mission trip with the church on Saturday. This will be the first year he will miss a mission trip. He has not said it, but I can see it is bothering him because he has been talking about old mission trips and the good memories from them. He went to help Julianne pack, which was hard for him. *He tweeted, "@NotJustAnnieBody been a long day of work but finally did the impossible...Got Julianne's suitcase packed #missiontrip2012"*

We are looking forward to June 21 when we leave to go with our high school youth group to Panama City Beach for camp. Jay will be the paramedic for the trip; I will be a counselor. Trey will be a part of the group, and Collin gets to enjoy being the little brother of the group. The doctors know how important this is to Trey; almost as important as Hawaii. We will be staying a week after to enjoy the beach.

There are two events coming up we are supporting Pray for Trey: On June 15, the Pray for Trey Beale Street Pub Crawl is being held beginning at 6 p.m. Why we would approve this type of event? All participants must purchase a Pray for Trey t-shirt. We want to be able to share God's word through this event. Our family feels God will be honored by having us sharing His word with the people, even if it is by selling a t-shirt.

In Mark 6, Jesus returns to his hometown of Nazareth. This is also when He sends the twelve disciples out to do His work.   In Mark 6:34 at the feeding of the 5,000, scripture says, *"When Jesus went ashore, He saw a large crowd, and He felt compassion for them because they were like sheep without a shepherd; and He began to teach them many things."* Just as Trey has mentioned in his testimony, the power of tweeting scripture or sharing the story of Trey's struggle could prompt someone to ask about the power of God. There will be people there ready to teach them about the love of Christ!

On June 30 there will be a Pray for Trey bike ride held at Germantown Baptist Church. If you are not going to ride, please feel free to come and enjoy the fun beginning at 7 a.m. There will be several distances rides, a family ride, and other activities.

June 2, 2012

We were able to attend the Relay for Life sponsored by the American Cancer Society on Saturday night. Trey was honored to stand next to Jim Siegfried, the honorary chairman. Jim coached Trey in basketball with his daughter, Tara, when our boys, Trey and Corbin were probably in 2nd grade. Jim had a major spiritual impact on Trey, even as a basketball coach. When Trey asked Jesus into his heart, we talked about who at the church would baptize him. He immediately said Coach Jim! This was around the time Jim was first diagnosed with cancer. God had begun a journey for Jim all his own. Now, 10 years later, Jim is our inspiration! Always giving glory and credit to God and leaning on His everlasting arms!

Jay and I were so overwhelmed by the Collierville support for Trey. Even though the evening was relatively cool for June, Trey was weak and could not stand for very long. We brought a chair for Trey and just let people come to him as Jay and I walked the track to read the luminaries donated in honor of Trey. Many of the donations came from our Collierville High School football family.

In order to begin the evening, Trey rode in the golf cart with Jim around the path laid out by the Relay for Life volunteers. This event goes all night long and Trey was lucky to last a little more than one hour.

"Mom, can we go now?" he asked. I stood next to him with a fan, but couldn't cool his body temperature.

Corbin, his friend, asked "Man, can I get you anything?"

"No man," answered Trey. "I'm fine."

I knew it was time to call it a day and Trey needed to rest.

June 3, 2012

Yesterday, we put Collin on the church bus to New Orleans. It was hard for us knowing how much Trey wanted to go. While at home, Trey did a lot of online shopping. I received a text, TREY: "Ok I'm about to get a G shock watch 60% off on finish line."
LISA: "Wow!"

He was so proud of the deal he received on his watch, with free shipping. We spent most of the day being lazy until I received a phone call from Tony Sarwar, an Alderman in Collierville. Tony had called yesterday because some of his basketball friends were hanging out at his house and he invited Trey to join the party. Trey was not feeling well so Tony said he would try back another time.

Later that evening, Tony told me he wanted to stop by the house to introduce a friend to Trey. Tony, a strength and life coach for many young athletes had been working with Jarnell Stokes, a member of the University of Tennessee basketball team, and he wanted to meet Trey. When I told Trey that Tony and Jarnell were coming by the house, he acted liked I had pumped him full of Red Bull.

They arrived and Jarnell brought the first framed autographed print Jarnell had made. They talked about basketball, tennis shoes, and more basketball. Then, Jarnell gave Trey a pair of his size 22 shoes. The young man has large feet! We spent time taking pictures with the "gentle giant" who loves the Lord. Tony brought his daughter and her friend who also wanted to meet Trey. It was so ironic. Trey was excited to talk with someone he had wanted to meet; and two sweet girls who had been praying for Trey were excited to meet him.

As we were talking, Tony dialed his phone and handed it to Trey. On the other end of the phone was Coach Cuonzo Martin of the University of Tennessee basketball team. I wish I had recorded the conversation. Coach Martin told Trey about his diagnosis of non-Hodgkin Lymphoma in 1997. They talked about the chemotherapy he endured and how he is now in remission. He was very encouraging to Trey.

When Tony and Jarnell were leaving, we found out Tony, newly engaged, had left his fiance to come spend time with our family. We quickly sent them out the door back to their engagement party. Trey's smile was permanent for hours; maybe days.

Trey tweeted, *"@JarnellStokes man thanks for stopping by and for the shoes. Ha I told you I had the same ones! Good luck in Brazil!"* And Trey posted a picture on Twitter of his shoes next to Jarnell's.

He followed with another tweet *"So blessed to meet Tony and Jarnell and speak with Coach Cuonzo (true inspiration). Ready to spend all day tom poolside! #G'nighttweeters."*

The next day, Trey hung the picture on the wall and posted it on Instagram with the caption *"Too blessed to have this hanging on my wall."*

It was nice to see D. J. Stephens post on Instagram, *"Ayo @jarnellstokes look..."*
Jarnell responded, *"@ddotjay that's my friend!"*

Common bonds between three people - love for the almighty round ball and love for the One that gave them the talent. My prayer is these young men with the talent will continue to keep giving God glory for what they have received. They are very blessed.

CHAPTER 19

HOW DOES GOD PREPARE YOU?

"Yet not My will, but Yours be done." Luke 22:42

June 5, 2012

When I didn't hear Trey during the night, the first thing I did when I woke up was check my phone. My sleeping is not really sleeping; it is more like cat naps. One of the first things I see is Trey's tweet this morning.

"Even though I had 0 sleep through the night...This makes me feel like I got too much sleep! #encouraged". He posted a picture from his daily devotion of June 5 which was marked up, underlined, and highlighted in at least five different colors.

Your Will Be Done

From A Shelter From the Storm

> *Many things come our way in life, unexpected disappointments, fiery ordeals, and often we cannot see the reason for them. But whether these are major or minor problems, we need to handle them all.*

> *The Lord's love for us is endlessly tender and encouraging. The things He allows to happen to us are always for our ultimate benefit. He wants us to trust where we cannot see. It is not a reckless leap in the dark, but sincere trust and faith that says, "I know for certain that God's will is best for me." This kind of faith leaves the choice up*

to God with the words that His Son taught us, "Your will be done."

Our faithful prayer every day must simply be, "Your will be done!" this is the only way in which we can get to know His peace. Then we will begin to understand how His perfect will functions; always for our good, even though it does not immediately appear so. It is a wonderful privilege and blessing to be able to testify that our will is yielded to God's perfect will.

His daily devotion made me think of how God had prepared Jay and me for this journey. At the beginning of the movie "Bruce Almighty", Bruce was driving in his car, praying for God to give him a sign, some sort of sign. Then, there came a flashing caution sign. He kept praying as he was speeding down the road and, out of nowhere, came a huge truck with STOP signs on the back, a blinking red light, and another caution sign. He swerved to miss the truck and ended up running into a pole. I wish all of God's warning signs were that clear!

At the age of 17, I lost my father to ALS, Lou Gehrig's disease. For six years, my mother carried a heavy burden of taking care of my father. I still lived at home but my two older sisters had married and moved out of the house. I matured very quickly during that time. I had no choice.

My father died December 27, 1982. I believe God had a purpose in the illness of my father and the state of our relationship because it made me who I am today.

Many years later, I married Jay. I had known him since he was in the second grade and God blessed our family when he decided to be a paramedic. Today, he is a City of

Memphis Firefighter/IV Certified Paramedic and also works in the Baptist Hospital Emergency Room.

Jay's younger brother, Barry, was diagnosed with Hodgkin's disease at age 16 in 1991. Barry was a St. Jude patient and also a patient of Dr. Tauer's. Barry passed away when Trey was 6 months old on December 27, 1996, the same day of the year my father died. People were drawn to Barry. People that have known both of them say Trey is so much like Barry. Barry loved the Lord. Before his death, he made sure no one blamed God for what he went through. Barry was 22 when he passed away, at home with the family by his side. That scene replays in my head, over and over, like it was yesterday.

In 2007, Jay's father, Jerry, was diagnosed with cancer in his sinuses that eventually spread. He was also treated by West Clinic. He had chemotherapy, but it didn't take long before the cancer spread. By February 13, 2008, we lost Papaw, a loss that devastated our family. To me, he became the father I never had, loving me unconditionally. At this point, we said "enough is enough." By then, my hatred for any disease was so great, I could not talk about it or be an advocate that anything could be cured.

Now, my son is 15 and fighting for his life. My questions are endless. But I believe God has prepared us for this specific moment in time. Certainly, we don't understand exactly what we are experiencing, but we are more prepared to handle now what we are going though because of what we experienced then.

When we ask why and we don't get direct answers immediately, we get impatient. God answers them in time. We have to remember His time is not our time. Sometimes, we don't like the answers. But He does answer.

Part of Trey's video testimony, when they asked us, "Have you ever asked yourself why us?" didn't air. I remember Jay and I looking and each other and saying, "No."

Trey answered, "Why not me?"

"Life is a tapestry: We are the warp; angels, the weft; God, the weaver.   Only the Weaver sees the whole design." Eileen Freeman

How blessed I am to have a husband that is a paramedic. I do all the scheduling, talking with doctors, blogging and organization of fundraisers, but there is nothing more important than the administration of the medications throughout the day. Lord, thank you for giving us exactly what we need, despite what we might ask for, and for all the years of preparation.

Jay and I have to prepare, not only Trey, but Collin. Trey has a firm grasp on what the Lord has prepared for him, either in heaven or here on earth. Trey is very worried that Collin doesn't understand his disease and that he will eventually go be with the Lord.

> *"Even children are known by the way they act, whether their conduct is pure, and whether it is right. Ears to hear and eyes to see— both are gifts from the Lord."* Proverbs 20:11-12

Trey once asked Collin if he was afraid of him dying. Collin said no. We don't know how much of "no" he truly grasps. We are praying God will prepare them and shelter their ears and eyes to exactly what they need to know. I have no doubts about Trey, even though he still struggles with questions, at times. We all do. But there is not a scripture that teaches me more to trust my faith than Matthew 19:17:

> *"Jesus said, "Why do you question me about what is good? God is the One who is good. If you want to enter the life of God, just do what he tells you."'*

It's so simple. Do what He says and He will prepare us. Easier said than done! We have something called our own will. We have to remember to give our will to Him daily. It will be hard for us to give the doctors total control of Trey's care when we see them. But we know God has gone before and prepared them. We have heard Kurt Tauer's testimony and he has a heart for God and his patients. We also know Dr. Sara Federico loves the Lord and Trey just as much and prays for him. We are praying that God has prepared their minds as one.

Please pray with us as we meet with the doctors at 3 p.m. Pray we leave understanding the future treatment and that this will be an encouraging visit for Trey. Trey is asking for pain pills quite often now. I can honestly say there are some things I am not prepared to hear. Maybe God has prepared me and I don't know it. May God be glorified in whatever He has in store for us.

"Whatever you ask in My name, that will I do, so that the Father may be glorified in the Son. If you ask Me anything in my name, I will do it." John 14:13

June 6, 2012

When Dr. Sara called me on my cell phone in the waiting area and asked if we could meet in the conference room without Trey, I knew it could not be good. They wanted to just discuss details and Trey does not like details. Trey likes to get to the bottom line and quick.

I knew, immediately, when we walked in the room something heavy was about to come down. We have met with these doctors so many times. We know their body language, the tone in their voice, and even their gestures. I felt the pressure in my chest; my heart began to race, and my hands were clammy.

They proceeded to tell us many facts. Trey's bilirubin has maintained a level of .2 or .3 for weeks. As of yesterday it was 2.8., a dramatic jump for his liver counts. We told them Trey went to the restroom and told Jay he needed to drink more water because his urine was changing colors. They also told us his white count is still up. We have been battling the white count for weeks with antibiotics trying to get it down to a decent level.

Two things were particularly concerning: Trey's tumor marker (CA19-9), which had decreased over the months had suddenly taken a jump up in the last week. Also, the biopsies of the duodenum confirmed live viable cancer cells that were not being killed by the current chemotherapy. The chemotherapy was not working.

The doctors didn't give us many options. Dr. Tauer said he rarely says no, but Trey is not a candidate for surgery. He also said, rarely has he ever seen anyone make it through this stage. In my mind, I was saying, "But you said, but you said...we could do this and that..."

They are planning to give Trey a lesser chemotherapy, Gemcitabine, which causes few side effects so he can enjoy his summer. This chemotherapy will work better on the duodendum, but will not cure the cancer. I was expecting them to say they were going to hook him up tomorrow and start this treatment. Instead, they told us it can wait until we get back from our Florida vacation. They also consulted with MD Anderson and this was their suggestion also. Surely they could get in at least one treatment before we leave in a little more than a week.

Dr. Tauer told us Trey's months will get tougher and he will become more fatigued, tired, and wanting to sleep. As Trey said, "like a typical teenager." Eventually, his liver will fail and he will just go to sleep. The doctors predict Trey will have a rough September and, at best, last until

December. I could not argue with what they were telling us because it is what they told us from the beginning, realistically. I just wanted to hold Trey and not let go. I asked God to make time stand still for me.

I reminded them God sets the parameters on death and we don't know when God has in mind to take Trey. They agreed. But I also said, in the meantime, we would follow their medical advice. Trey tweeted, *"Things can change in a blink of an eye, but knowing that it is nothing that my God can't handle, takes away all unnecessary worries!"*

I think Jay and I came home shocked from the doctor's visit. It was not what we expected. Even so, I can honestly say we are all okay. We are all very tired and just want to spend time together doing what we love to do. How can we worry when Trey is not worried?

Trey's main thought is getting to the beach and my bosses's house in North Carolina. Trey also has a bucket list and we are going to try to get to Disney World or Universal between now and the end of August. I know it is hot, but we don't care.

Since we now know a little more about how Trey is progressing, I am going to try to work a little to extend my leave. I cannot explain the regret I feel when I pull out of my drive each day, but I don't know how long I will need to be off in the future. I am so blessed by my employer, Burch, Porter & Johnson. I will never forget the day I received pictures from the friends in my office. There they stood on the front steps of our building, attorneys and staff with #prayfortrey t-shirts on, holding a sign that said "BPJ LOVES YOU!" I go from family at home to family at work.

Jay is still being covered his co-workers at the Memphis Fire Department. What an amazing testament to the men and women he works with! They are truly a brotherhood. They have collected money, brought food, and worked for him because they say, "Trey is like our son too." God bless them.

Tomorrow, Trey will be having a procedure at West Clinic. Because of his bilirubin levels being elevated, they believe the original stent in his bile duct is blocked. Dr. Hodgkiss will go in with a catheter through his side into his liver with dye to show the blockage. They will place another stent in his bile duct at this time. While they are doing this procedure, they will block his pancreas also. He has been complaining of back pain a lot. We hope these procedures will help. Since he had the duodenum stent put in, he has been able to eat with no problems. I know he is looking forward to Florida and good crab legs.

The majority of Trey's friends are on the mission trip in New Orleans. I know he wishes he had them here to talk to them about this situation. Collin is also on the trip and we are praying Collin does not hear any of the information regarding the visit with the doctors until we can talk with him. We will handle it when he gets home.

Right now, I can honestly say I feel empty, for probably the first time since the beginning of this journey. Yes, Jesus turned water into wine and my God is a mighty God. But all I can muster is to ask for a glass of unsweet tea please, with a little extra ice.

June 8, 2012

We have been very busy the last couple of days. I have had to ask Jay what happened the day before just to make sure I have kept everything straight in my mind. It has been quite a roller coaster, so get ready to jump on and ride for a minute.

Tuesday, June 5, we met with Dr. Tauer from West Clinic, Dr. Sara (Federico), and Karen Williams from St.

Jude and scheduled the Thursday procedure to insert the catheter to open the bile duct.

Wednesday was to be a relaxing day by the pool. But, Trey woke up with a fever of 101.5. He begged me not to call St. Jude, nothing new with Trey. He must believe the fever will magically go away, but we had no option. Trey has been receiving Levaquin by his port for days. They wanted to give him another antibiotic so we headed to St. Jude.

Thankfully, they already had decided the antibiotic and were waiting for us. They drew blood for cultures to determine infection and to see his counts. We met with an infectious disease doctor to cover all areas from toenails to port infections. During this time we received his counts back and his bilirubin had increased to 4.4. The previous blood count was 2.8, all the more important reason to have the procedure on Thursday.

West Clinic called while we were at St. Jude and requested we come Wednesday afternoon to have a CT scan done. My cellphone kept cutting in and out as Dr. Hodgkiss was trying to explain the reasons for having this done. This would alleviate having it done prior to the procedure Thursday morning. It was around noon and we asked if we could eat before we came because we had not eaten all day. An empty stomach equals a grumpy Trey. In most houses the saying goes, "When mama ain't happy, nobody's happy." In our house, well…. We had to be at West Clinic at 3 p.m.

Our initial plans for the day had been to go to Perkins for breakfast, so we just kept our plans and went to Perkins for lunch. Trey had a five stack of pancakes and ate every bite WITH bacon. The kid is having no problem eating. It was such a great time at lunch to relax and for all three of us stuff our faces, something we are all good at doing.

We were in and out at West Clinic and came home to family helping us rearrange furniture and eating dinner. About 9:30 p.m. our home phone, which we rarely answer, rang. I looked at caller id and it said KURT TAUER. We were not expecting this call. Roller coaster ride downhill now.... Dr. Tauer said if tomorrow's procedure didn't work, we had two options:

1. Do nothing. Trey would have, at best, four to five weeks to live. His liver would start to fail. He would get tired and just go to sleep.

2. Have surgery on Friday to resect the duodenum section and repair the bile duct area, a very difficult surgery to survive. Dr. Tauer didn't doubt Trey would survive the surgery but had doubts about Trey being able to come home from the hospital.

He put it all on the line. We had to make the decision Wednesday night. We all agreed Trey should make the final decision. Dr. Tauer told us to pray about it and just let him know what we decided. I was shaking the entire time I was talking with Dr. Tauer on the phone because I would need to take all this information to Trey. After discussing it with Trey, he said he wanted the surgery. It was the best decision to give him a little more time. We know he is tough.

"Can you get Collin home?" he asked, immediately. "And Julianne, Tim, Hunter and Cody?"

Collin was still in New Orleans on the church mission trip. Jay immediately called Keith Cochran and his wife, Bretta, and called his mother. They were at our home within minutes. We began to make plans to get the kids home from the church mission trip in New Orleans.

Keith blurted out, "I'll drive and go get them." Keith had a very bad migraine and was on his knees in Trey's room.

"You are not driving anywhere," I said.

Jay's mother suggested we fly them home. Keith began calling the parents and checking flights while we all remained with Trey in his room.

In New Orleans, Ron Norton gathered Julianne, Tim, Hunter and Cody together and got them on speaker phone with Trey.

"Hey, you guys all there?" asked Trey. "I'm having surgery and it's pretty serious. Basically, I could die and I want my best friends to be here if it happens. I love ya'll and I just wanna know, would ya'll come home early for me?"

Ron had not told them what was going on. I am sure there was shock on their faces and in their conversation after Trey got off the phone. After talking to the kids, we didn't have time to fly them home. Keith spent hours calling parents to tell them plans had changed because of many logistic problems. Bretta and another friend would drive to New Orleans EARLY Thursday morning to pick up the kids and bring them home. What a blessing.

During this time, Trey had been experiencing excruciating back pain and was asking for his next pain pill often. The doctors believe that the pain was from the pressure of the cyst. The pseudocyst had grown 50% since the duodenum stent had been placed last Thursday. This was putting pressure on everything and pushed this stent up to the bile duct, closing everything off. The doctors were amazed Trey was still eating, not nauseated or throwing up. I told Dr. Tauer about him eating the five pancakes and he laughed. They didn't know how bile was passing through.

Before we left for West Clinic, Trey sent me a text with a picture of his devotion and a portion highlighted. *"Therefore, hold onto His promises, place your entire trust and faith in the living Christ. Through Him you will survive all dangers and adversity."*

We left for West Clinic with Trey in such pain he could not stand up straight. I pushed him in a wheelchair into West Clinic. Dr. Hodgkiss explained the procedure to us. Originally, we thought he would be doing a block on the pancreas. But, like Dr. Tauer, he believed the pain was from the cyst and bile duct area. Dr. Hodgkiss acted like this was no big deal and treated this procedure like any other, which calmed me a great deal.

I held Trey's hand and prayed over him before he went into the procedure. Jay and I loved on him and were able to go into the room where they were doing the procedure for a while. Actually, one of us could have stayed, but we both opted to wait outside where we could observe through a large window and watch every step on a computer. It was amazing to watch the needle puncture the cyst and see the catheter being placed.

Dr. Hodgkiss came out after 45 minutes or so and told us everything went great. He is one tough kid, with his new G shock watch still on his wrist. He drained the cyst, full of clear fluid consisting of pancreatic enzymes, into the stomach. It was not full of cancer cells. He also placed the catheter in Trey's chest, which was Trey's choice. This catheter goes in and down along the duodenum stent and opened up the bile duct above. Trey's bile began to flow immediately into the bag!

Trey came out of the procedure with 102.7 fever. I asked the nurses if Dr. Tauer would let him leave West Clinic with fever and she didn't know. He was burning up and sleeping from the procedure. Dr. Hodgkiss frequently checked him. Trey would wake, drink a little and fall back asleep. The doctor, nurses, and technicians were remarking how Trey would talk during the procedure and apologize for flinching in pain. They told us we have the most polite son! They also said, "Most patients we have curse us out for that." Hearing that makes a mama proud, even if he was on drugs.

Dr. Tauer finally came in. Dr. Hodgkiss decided to go back in next Thursday and have a size 10 catheter inserted to cut down on the chances of the bile getting blocked in the catheter. It will not be nearly like the procedure he just experienced. And, Dr. Hodgkiss will internalize the catheter at that time. We thought we would have to cancel the vacation but, now, we are back on! He will also go ahead with the block next week on his pancreas because his back is still bothering him.

I had to ask Dr. Tauer why the gloom and doom the night before. Today, we feel Dr. Hodgkiss saved Trey's life. Dr. Tauer explained he has to always give the whole picture in case the procedure didn't work? We still have to watch Trey over the weekend for signs of infection.

Trey is ONE in five million since the 1970's to have adult pancreatic adenocarcinoma. These statistics are astounding. Dr. Tauer reminded me that he told us from the beginning that he did not have a crystal ball and only God knew the answers. I told him that he knew who we relied on - God. I told him we will definitely rely on him because we know who he relies on. He said he could not do it any other way, but sometimes we have to wait to listen for God. Dr. Tauer told us we have to be patient. He said we do not need surgery right now, might not ever need surgery. But we need to take one thing at a time. What a lesson for our family from our doctor. Wait for God and listen.

We left West Clinic with Trey walking out and no fever. Our God is good! We are so blessed to have a doctor who will talk about his faith and loves the Lord. We were also blessed to have Jim Siegfried there with us during the waiting time. Jim was able to be there when Dr. Hodgkiss came out and gave us the good news. It has been funny when Jim has come to West Clinic during each procedure. We never know who he is going to tell the front desk he is in order to get to us in the back. Usually, they only allow family, but, to us, Jim is family. He has stood with us and looked over the doctor's shoulders as they have explained scans, procedures, and test results. Put a white coat on Jim and he would fit right in at West Clinic.

Trey came home and he was very sore. He explained the pain like he had been punched in the stomach. Oh, wait, but we went by Sonic before we went home because he was starving. About 9 p.m., Collin and the kids rolled in from the mission trip. We were all so glad to see them! It was around 10:30 p.m. and they all announced they were spending the night.

"Well, okay," I agreed. "As long as Trey sleeps in his bed since he did have a procedure today!" I just went to bed exhausted.

God provided a friend to text me for coffee this morning. I said, sure, but can you add donuts to for six teens? During our visit, she mentioned she was reading The Screwtape Letters, by C.S. Lewis. In the book, the devil has demons play on Christians to discourage them from their faith. In the book, *"(God) wants men to be concerned with what they do; our business is to keep them thinking about what will happen to them."* This is exactly the temptation we are fighting, worrying about tomorrow. Trey is very worried about us. But God reassures us in His word. *"Therefore do not worry for tomorrow; for tomorrow will care for itself. Each day has enough trouble of its own." Matthew 6:34*

I go back to what to Dr. Tauer said. We need to listen more to God, not be worried about the statistics, remember who our trust is in, and take care of today! Yes, Seize the Day! That's what Trey is doing!

Today, he has no fever. He emptied his bag around 4 a.m. By 10 a.m., after talking with Dr. Hodgkiss, we capped his bag and threw it away. The internal drain had begun to work. He immediately started working on his simple bucket list with his friends.

They built a pillow/blanket fort in our playroom. The adults had fun watching and taking pictures of the progress. Cindy and I got up under the fort and lay down with the kids and talked about the mission trip. It was precious time. Then, without warning, Trey stormed the room with silly string.

Later in the day, Jay took a crew to his fire station and they headed to Jerry's Sno Cone. The guys at the station were glad to see him. More than anything, Trey is glad his brother is home. Trey tweeted "Even if @collinerwin33 thinks I'm the worst big bro ever, I love him to death! #nohomo" And Trey posted a picture of the two of them from our trip to Knoxville. I am not sure Collin understands the emotional depth of the love Trey has for him.

We are keeping an eye on Trey for the next couple of days for fever, color, pain, etc. Otherwise, we are concentrating on each day to live it to the fullest. *"Whether, then, you eat or drink or whatever you do, do all to the glory of God." 1 Corinthians 10:31*

Roller coaster still on the tracks, slowing down a little to give these passengers a rest, if just for a day. . .our plans are to seize it! Don't wait until the roller coaster stops. It may be too late. Seize YOUR day!

June 11, 2012

Remember the roller coaster I talked about? We are still riding. We are going up hill right now.

Saturday morning at 3:25 a.m. I received a text:

TREY: "Mom you awake? Can I please have a small bowl of oatmeal? I can't go back to sleep and I have pills up here. The last thing I had was half a bowl of Cheesy jambalaya and I've used the bathroom 2 and now I'm starving."

LISA: "I'll get it. Kinda sounds good to me."

TREY: "You sure? You not sleepy?"

LISA: "Nope, I'm fine."

If my son wanted to eat, there was no way I was going to deny him or tell him I was sleepy. We enjoyed oatmeal sitting in his bed at 3:30 a.m. in the morning. After he ate, I told him to go to sleep.

Sunday morning, Trey woke up with a fever hovering a little over 99. Otherwise, Trey felt fine. He was exhausted from over-doing it the previous days, but he felt fine. Monday morning he woke up with 99.9 temperature. Getting close to the 100 degree mark scared me. I sent a text to Dr. Hodgkiss at West Clinic to discuss his pain and fever. He suggested Trey go ahead and have the procedure, originally scheduled for Thursday, tomorrow morning at 6:30 a.m. He will also have a nerve block in his pancreas. After being discharged from St. Jude in March, he received a block. They can last for many months. He will have another one to see if this will take care of the pain in his back. We pray this is why his back is hurting. My mind can only wonder about the different reasons why his back is hurting, but I don't want to go there because nothing has shown up. Next week, they'll internalize the catheter. A scab will form within 24 hours. He'll be able to swim and head to Florida on Thursday, June 21.

There are so many things on the table to schedule, and our timetable may not be God's timetable. Trey tweeted on Monday morning, *"I endure everything for people who are chosen by God so they experience salvation in Jesus with eternal glory. 2 Timothy 2:10 @LisaErwin13"*

"Be still, and know that I am God! I will be honored by every nation. I will be honored throughout the world." *Psalm 46:10*

CHAPTER 20

LAST WEST CLINIC PROCEDURE

"Pray in the Holy Spirit on all occasions with all kinds of prayers."
Ephesians 6:18

Tuesday morning, June 12 at 2:32 a.m. Trey sent me a text:

TREY: "Trey tiene mucha hambre."

LISA: "Si."

TREY: "Do you know what I said?"

LISA: "You can't eat. You can only drink."

TREY: "What can I drink? I just know that when I get up in the morn I'll be cramping like CRAZY cause of my empty stomach not to mention how much bile my stomach emptied today is gonna make it worse. So not even one pack of those tiny gummies Mrs. Melissa brought?"

LISA: "Nope. Can't eat. You can drink Gatorade."

TREY: "What makes me mad the most is my stomach was hurting around midnight so I figured I didn't have to force any food but now I'm about to die."

LISA: "You are not about to die. Gatorade will help."

We kept texting back and forth about eating versus drinking and he asked if we would eat breakfast after the procedure and I told him we would go to Perkins. He thought that was awesome.

LISA: "Honey, sleep."

Having labs drawn is always the first thing we do at West Clinic and St. Jude. His bilirubin came back as .6, very good. Dr. Hodgkiss saw no need to change the drain. In the procedure room, Dr. Hodgkiss saw, on the ultrasound, the cyst had returned to a very large size. He drained the cyst and removed around 120 milliliters. The next step was to get Trey more awake so they could proceed with the block.

The block is performed in a room with a CT scan. Before Dr. Hodgkiss did the block, the scan showed the cyst still there. It did not make sense to send Trey home without knowing if his pain was from this cyst or his pancreas. Dr. Hodgkiss agreed to flip Trey over and drain the cyst through the stomach after he did the block. I was able to be with Trey during the procedure. Trey is one tough guy. Dr. Hodgkiss was able to drain another 90 milliliters off the cyst for it to disappear. Trey was VERY hungry – a good sign!

Trey came out of the procedure and was in recovery talking to us in a very drug- induced state. I am so thankful I have this on video. We were trying to get him situated and he lifted the covers and looked down toward his feet and then looked at me with this serious look on his face.

"Whoa," he said," that looks nasty. Is that from me?"

The nurse answered, "We'll get you a clean blanket. It's from the drain."

"What do you need?" asked Dustin.

"A clean blanket," said the nurse

"It looks like I do-do'd myself," said Trey, "on the front."

We all lost it in the recovery area. It took everyone a minute to stop laughing and realize it was betadine still on his abdomen. Because of the hole(s) punctured in his stomach, Dr. Hodgkiss asked us to wait two hours before he ate. We made our usual trip after to Perkins and had lunch with Coach O'Neill. Trey had his five stack of pancakes. Trey tweeted after the procedure, *"Man that needle felt amazing going into my back 13cm that many times! #betterwork #luckynumber #sarcasm."* Then, he posted a picture I took of him on the table with the needle in his back.

Even though he was sore, he continued to feel better. He described the feeling of having a steel rod in his back, from the the needles. We have plans to go back Tuesday of next week to have the drain internalized after the liver has matured around it. He does have a little nausea, but had a lot of pain medications yesterday with no nausea medications.

Unfortunately, he woke up this morning with 101.8 temperature. He really felt good and had so much on his plate he wanted to do. He is trying to knock things off his bucket list. I think we just don't have the right antibiotic yet. Right now, Jay and Trey are at St. Jude with the doctor trying to figure out what antibiotic would be best, drawing labs, probably seeing if the infectious disease doctor needs to come back in. I promised him he would not be there all day and he would be able to get things done and go to church tonight.

I pray we find the right antibiotic or the source of the fever. Actually I'd love to find both. Trey is counting the hours until Florida next week. It is a place he knows well and feels he can relax. Trey is looking forward to worshiping with his friends and, then, spending a week with his family. If the fever continues, he might not go anywhere.

Psalms 18:30-36
As for God, His way is blameless;
The word of the Lord is tried;
He is a shield to all who take refuge in Him.
For who is God, but the Lord?
And who is a rock, except our God,
The God who girds me with strength
And makes my way blameless?
He makes my feet like hinds' feet,
And sets me upon my high places.

He trains my hands for battle,
So that my arms can bend a bow of bronze.
You have also given me the shield of Your salvation,
And Your right hand upholds me;
And Your gentleness makes me great.
You enlarge my steps under me,
And my feet have not slipped.

June 14, 2012

The days could be much harder if we didn't have Trey and Collin's humor. Trey tweets, *"When you are holding a box of spaghetti noodles and the bottom breaks open and noodles are everywhere."* All we could do was laugh at noodles in the pantry floor as the dogs went nuts and Trey stood there with the box in his hand. I was not going to clean it up.

The doctors decided to watch Trey and his fever for a couple of days while his cultures are growing. Now it has been 24 hours and nothing has grown for a bacterial infection. They will give it at least 48 hours.

Dr. Sara called this morning. Trey's fever was 101.1, but he felt fine. She asked for the home health nurse to take more blood for a special blood culture test to check for a specific infection. Dr. Sara's fear is Trey's fever will spike while we are out of town and we will need to get back to St. Jude as soon as possible. At least we don't have to run to St. Jude right now.

Trey's fever usually spikes early in the morning. He takes two Advil and the fever goes away without additional Advil throughout the day. Dr. Sara mentioned a "cancer fever" but Trey is definitely not sick enough for that.

Last night, I could not sleep because my tooth was hurting. He says he does not sleep so I decided to check on him and see if he wanted to chat. He was sound asleep! It took me five minutes of fumbling with remotes to figure out how to turn off his television. It was a peaceful sleep and made my heart smile. It reminded me of the song our friend, Barry Delk, sang at Christmas,

"Go to sleep, my son. Go and chase your dreams.
This world can wait for one more moment.
Go and sleep in peace."

Of course, he told his dad he was awake during those hours. I said NO WAY!

We are continuing to pray the fever will go away or they will find the source of this infection. I did ask yesterday and was told there are times they NEVER find the source. With all we have been though, fever does not alarm me. I guess I should play mama gorilla and go to check his toenails to see if he has been clipping them again!

A week from today we will be leaving for Florida. We know God has it in His plans for us to make the trip without any hiccups. St. Jude is already preparing to send medications to the two different locations we will be staying.

I cannot tell you what new respect I have for parents with children with cancer. I never realized what my mother-in-law went through. I remember asking her a few years ago how she did it. If I remember her correctly, she told me it took a lot of faith and a whole lot of prayers. I don't remember seeing her get angry or lash out. She always had it together and knew the schedule from day to day. Now, I know she had the right to get angry at times and cry when alone. She had the right to be astounded at remarks made by other people. Until others walk in our shoes, there is no way to compare the anguish, hurt, desperation, guilt, and overflowing love you feel for your child. Satan steps in and tempts Jay and me on a daily basis to remind us of our flesh. Yet I am to live without an offendable spirit. I am so thankful I can, in confidence, tell him to get behind me. He has no power over me, my family, or my children! One day, in glory, I will thank Jesus for the ability to put Satan in his place by the blood of the cross.

June 15, 2012

Trey tweeted today, *"All people were created on this earth for one reason, to go and make disciples. Not just the ones who have a certain disease. So…"* Well said son.

We thought we could make it two days in a row without seeing a doctor but, Trey's drain began to leak last night. We are on our way to West Clinic to see what they can do. He is upset he could not make it to tacky day at Vacation Bible School! Maybe we can. My fear is he would not dress up but decided to show his drain as his tacky dress!

Trey now has a size 10 drain in his abdomen. At this point, explaining why the change was needed would need a medical book. We are just glad it is working. We are also praising God for no fever today! The cyst is back. We will deal with it on Tuesday when they plan to internalize the drain.

I believe Trey needed to remind everyone about who his inspiration is, so he tweeted, *"…don't call me an inspiration cause I'm only doing what you were also told to do. So if you do this you can inspire (make disciples) also."*

We all got a surprise on Saturday. I received an email and video message to Trey from Jeremy Camp. Jeremy knows the pain and suffering of cancer. He lost his first wife to ovarian cancer. He has since remarried and his family is praying for ours. Trey tweeted *"Thanks @jeremycamp for the encouraging message! I appreciate your prayers @LisaErwin13"* The lyrics from Jeremy's song "Walk by Faith" describe our journey. *"Well I will walk by faith, even when I cannot see; because this broken road prepares Your will for me."*

June 17, 2012

Happy Father's Day! This morning, Trey was dressed in his blue polo with his purple polo bow tied and ready for church. I can honestly say Jay is an awesome dad to both our sons! I am blessed and so are they.

Trey has had a rough weekend. His back pain has continued to get worse. I believe this is the cyst pressing on something and everything. This pain has truly affected Trey. He cannot get comfortable in any position. I am thankful though, he has not been running any fever. That's a blessing.

Trey was not able to sit through church today because of the pain which has caused the nausea to return. We are so blessed to have Dr. Sara at St. Jude who genuinely cares and prays for us. She sent me a text during church to check on Trey. I told her about his pain and she immediately doubled his pain medications (two oxycodone every four hours) with the phenergan, ativan and steroids- plus many other medications. He began to feel a little better and said the pain was manageable. I could tell by his attitude.

People in pain don't want to talk or participate in really anything. I know Trey has been pushing it the last couple of days to try to do things with friends to be a part of "the group", but I am praying they will be the kind of friends that know how to extend grace to someone that is handling pain under difficult circumstances and still love their friend.

Tomorrow we go to St. Jude to get the monthly antibiotic for pneumonia and make the pain medication adjustments for his back. We will discuss the upcoming month's schedule and treatment. I cannot wait to tell them Trey got on the scale last night and weighed 115! We know his red blood count is going down, which is not good. It is not time for a blood transfusion, but I know we will talk about it.

Tuesday we will go to West Clinic for another procedure. He will have his drain internalized and the duodenum stent extended. This has been the plan all along. One additional thing he might need is to have an internal stent/drain put in the cyst so it continually drains into the pancreas. Dr. Hodgkiss will try to perform this on Tuesday. This will be the only way to keep the cyst draining. We need to have this procedure be successful. If anyone can do it, West Clinic can!

On Wednesday, Trey's dream will come true. He will meet DeAngelo Williams, his top all-time favorite football player. We had University of Memphis season tickets all the years he played and Trey has followed him all his years with the Carolina Panthers. I don't think I have talked to a friendlier young man. He wants to make sure the time they spend together is not focused on cancer or DeAngelo's football career. He wants it to be just two guys hanging and talking about guy things, girls, etc. Our family looks forward to this time on Wednesday. Trey even went as far to say this is almost as good as his Make a Wish. He will go skeet shooting with Jay, Collin, and Coach O'Neill. This is something Trey has never done and DeAngelo will teach him.

Thursday we leave for Florida. By Thursday, my prayer list will be a mile long for this trip - shipping of medications, the High School church trip, our family vacation, etc. We will cross that bridge later in the week.

This last week literally wore Jay and me out. I still have many things to do before we leave. I was so exhausted on Friday, I was in tears. We get weary physically and mentally. Last week, I worked three days. People tell us they don't know how we are doing it. Trust me, every step I am taking I am praying I can take the next. I know Trey's prayer is 10 fold. I am brought back to the passage in *Isaiah 40:31 "They that wait upon the Lord will renew their strength; they will mount up as eagles with wings. They will run and not grow weary. They will walk and not faint."*

Many times, I have relied upon this verse and gained strength. But I know I needed to rest. God is faithful to continue to give strength to our family. We will continue to thank Him for everything He is doing for us.

After the last couple of weeks and being told so many things and Trey having to experience one procedure after another, we are so thankful for His hand on Trey.

Jay commented the other day when we had plans for something and he laughed and said, "Isn't it just like God, we should know better to plan when He knows the plans."

So even though we know the plans of our busy week, we will rest in the fact God is in control and we will be at peace with what God is going to do.

Tim Few's Thoughts: Trey and I had been talking a couple of weeks before we left for Florida about him and Julianne. We were trying to figure out a way for me to get ordained to marry them on the beach. We even decided we would wear the same suits. I found out I could get ordained online. There was only one problem, you had to be 18 to get ordained and I was not 18. We almost had everyone convinced. It was fun for us to attempt to make it work.

CHAPTER 21

FLORIDA HERE WE COME!

"Therefore humble yourselves under the mighty hand of God, that He may exalt you at the proper time." 1 Peter 5:6

On Saturday, June 21, we hit the road in a rental car arranged by Jim Siegfried. We knew we would not be able to ride in one of our vehicles to carry some of the medications, even though some were being sent by FedEx to the high school retreat center. We needed to make sure we had a vehicle where Trey would be comfortable. Jay, Trey, Collin, Julianne and I hit the road and made it to Panama City that evening. Some of the tech crew drove down the same day, but were staying at a different hotel. We made arrangements to meet, eat come crab and play in the arcades. I think they got the better end of the hotel deal. *Trey tweeted, "Taking on this 5 star hotel wit @NotJusAnnieBody! We got this...Oh wait... Is that a spider...#craphotel"* Needless to say, we all slept in our clothes on top of the bedspreads. When I woke up the next morning, Julianne was next to me with her hoodie on her head, afraid something would crawl on her. We could not get out of there fast enough.

> **Julianne Shiles' Thoughts:** Church camp at the beach was different, but it still didn't take away Trey's sense of humor. I remember when we were singing one of the worship songs and Trey was so tired and he was hurting. We thought the song would never end. Trey said "Oh my gosh" and finally gave

up and sat down. We stayed in Florida an extra week and Trey said he was going to have crab every day and he didn't care how it made him feel.

We met up with the church crew and got our room assignments. Trey was in a room with his buddies for the week. At the beginning of the week, Trey realized Cody Jordan forgot his bible. Trey gave him his bible and told him he was not going to need it because he had another bible he used to highlight. The bible he gave to Cody is the bible he received when he moved into the student ministry in 6th grade.

We knew we were going to share the week with another church, Crossgates Baptist from Brandon, Mississippi. This thrilled my heart because their leader is Ryan Mullins who served as Trey's junior high minister at Germantown Baptist. It was going to be great spending a week with Ryan and Anne. Ryan and Keith were sensitive to our needs and gave Jay and me a preview of the video series, "Not A Fan", that the youth would be studying for the week. The study deals with the main character having a near death experience as he embarks on his spiritual journey. During the preview, I was in the back with Ryan.

I looked at him, in tears, and said, "This will be the last time he is here."

"I know", said Ryan, as he hugged me.

Trey was not able to spend much time in the sessions. The chairs were the small metal chairs. When he came, he brought his pillows and sat for as long as he could. During one worship set, I stood in the back and watched everyone stand with their hands in the air. Trey was sitting in his chair, worshipping with his hands in the air and Julianne by his side.

His goal for his Florida vacation was to get as much sun as he could. During free time, he would lay on the beach unashamed of his thin body with puncture wounds from previous procedures. For some reason, he could not even burn. I suppose it was from all of his medications. I stayed in contact with Dr. Tom Hodgkiss the entire time. Trey had some swelling and I sent a picture to Tom. He thought it was from all the poking and prodding he did on Trey during the procedure just before we left. We just cannot get him to eat. He is blaming it on camp food.

Trey had a new lifeproof case for his phone. How else do you see if your lifeproof case works unless you video yourself under water? His lungs were in great shape because he used his phone to video plenty of people at the pool under water.

A tropical storm was looming and the church decided to head home early on Monday. We decided to head to the condominium we had rented for the next week to be with our family. It was a good time with the church as we worshipped God together. He showed up in a big way.

Hunter Byer and Julianne joined our entire family for the next week in Florida (June 26-30). Our goal was to eat, shop, and lay on the beach. We had perfect weather. The tropical depression passed over and left the beach nice and cool.

We went out to eat for my mother's 82nd birthday and Trey had all the crab he could eat. I overheard Trey say, "Watch this," before taking a picture of a white napkin. The next thing I know, the picture was on Instagram and the kids were dying laughing. Trey was up to his tricks again. People began to comment on his napkin picture thinking Trey was throwing in the towel calling it his "White Flag". He simply posted a picture of a napkin from our restaurant.

It actually stirred up quite a conversation on Instagram. In Florida, it had us rolling on the floor.

"They actually think I'm going to give up," Trey said.

I begged him to let me respond to some of the comments and he said, "No, No Mom!"

I didn't agreed with what he did, but kids will be kids. I guess he got his payback because the crab he had for dinner didn't agree with him. Tom (Dr. Hodgkiss) told us crab is actually one of the hardest foods for the pancreas to digest. Trey didn't like hearing that news. His pain has started to increase and he has not been able to sleep.

On Wednesday, Jay and I rented a big boat for all our family and friends. So many were in Panama City on vacation, so it worked out just perfect to have the Wylie's, the Wakefield's, and the Newman's join our family. We snorkeled, found sand dollars, jumped off the side of the boat into the bay, watched the dolphins play, and even had a hula hoop contest. I know the day wore Trey out because he fell asleep down in the galley of the boat, but not before I got a picture of him trying to hula hoop! The sun was finally getting to him. But he said he had such a good time. He tweeted, *"Party boat time! @NotJusAnnieBody @whbyer12 @rathorn90 @leighton_newman @stacia_stonebrook @sarah_wylie"*

As the wonderful day on the boat turned to evening, Trey's pain increased and he complained of having problems breathing. I sent a text to Tom, telling him we needed to set up an appointment to see him and Dr. Tauer as soon as we get back. He had never had trouble breathing and it frightened me.

Thursday, we arranged to have our pictures taken by a professional photographer after dinner. We ate at The Back Porch and Trey didn't eat a bite. While we were taking the pictures, we knew he was in pain. He would crouch down on his knees to relieve the pain in his abdomen. He was such a sport about the whole ordeal. He and Julianne had some incredible pictures made, as did he and his friends.

Trey, Hunter and Julianne decided to stay in on Friday. Trey's pain was such we kept him medicated all day so he could rest. They watched movies most of the day. Trey did try to lay by the pool for a little sun, but ended up back in the bed. I contacted Tom again to tell him Trey's pain was getting worse and he was complaining of his back hurting. Tom had already talked to Dr. Tauer and they were scheduling Trey for tests when we returned from Florida.

June 30, 2012

I have watched his abdomen continue to enlarge as the days have passed. Thursday night and Friday night he would kneel next to the bed because that was the only way he could get relief from the pain in his back and stomach. At times, we did tease about "his baby". Trey has a sense of humor, but it has worn off. About 4 a.m. this morning Trey woke me up and asked if he could have more pain medication.

"Honey, we just gave you your dose of medications within the last two hours", I answered.

"But Mom," he said, "it's not working." And he went back to kneel next to his bed and lean over the edge.

I woke Jay up and told him we could not wait any longer; Trey needed to get to the hospital. They would be able to give him intravenous pain medications for some relief. Maybe it would last until we got home. I only woke my sister, Donna, to tell her we were going to the hospital for some pain management. We took him to Gulf Coast Medical Hospital this morning. Trey didn't want to be there.

The staff at Gulf Coast Medical could not have been nicer. They immediately administered Dilaudid for his pain and phenergan. They did a full body CT scan due to the distention of his stomach. To my surprise, his cancer had spread. The doctors at the hospital explained the cancer has spread to his omentum, a layer or fold of tissue between the abdomen and the organs in your body.

What the radiologist said in Panama City (in Lisa words):

1. Numerous low density hepatic (liver) lesions presumed to be hepatic metastasis. No, we don't know if there are more liver lesions since the last scan. We will have to wait for St. Jude to read the scan.

2. Complex stent and drain system...but I see no specific evidence of occlusion or obstruction. In other words, great job Dr. Tom Hodgkiss.

3. Abdominal and pelvic ascites. This is excess fluid.

4. Probable omental metastasis. Here is where I mentioned the cancer has spread. The omentum is a large fatty structure and the radiologist suspects metastasis in the anterior abdomen. I will know so much more after St. Jude reads his scan. This is a place in the body with many small blood vessels.

5. Probable constipation. I think so! I talked to Dr. Hodgkiss today and he didn't think this was such a bad report. I love to hear encouraging word from our doctors. He thinks Trey is dealing with a lot of constipation.

6. Possible bone met in the right hemi pelvis. They have said this before but have always come back to tell us it is not cancer, but some other kind of shadow or something.

The doctors have told us there is nothing they can do for us and we need to get back to St. Jude as soon as possible. How do we get back as soon as possible? Trey is angry and wants to stay at the beach. We are trying to explain we need to get him to the hospital that can care for him. Gulf Coast Medical Hospital is trying to get Trey home by air or ground ambulance. As soon as I put that on Facebook, I had people from all walks of life calling and offering their planes. Unfortunately, after seven hours in the emergency room, it has become more vital we get a plane close to Panama City.

I have been on the phone with Dr. Sara and West Clinic all morning and they are all very saddened by our news. St. Jude already has a room for him. He does not want to leave Florida, but he has no choice. I am boarding the air ambulance with Trey. Jay will return to the condominium to pack the family and drive back to Memphis as soon as possible.

Trey was glued to his phone. He received a text from D. J. Stephens, "How are you little bro?" Trey replied, "Awful" D. J. said, "Dang, What's going on my guy?" And by that time, we were leaving for the airport.

July 1, 2012

Trey and I were flown by Lifeguard International, based in Pensacola, from Panama City to Memphis then transported, by ambulance, to St. Jude. It is such a blessing Trey does not remember any of the flight. Oh, how God protects the ones He loves. Trey was very lethargic on the plane and his breathing was very shallow. Alarms would go off on the machines hooked up to Trey and I would look at the nurse with panic on my face. They noticed his oxygen level had dropped and they decided they had to fly at a lower altitude in order to keep his oxygen level up. His blood pressure was up and the nurse on the plane asked if it was normally this high. I told her no. Flying at a lower altitude helped, but it felt like we were going two miles an hour. All I could do was look at my watch knowing how much time they told me it would take to get to Memphis. The nurse picked up on my anxiety and she began to start a conversation.

When we landed in Memphis and got off the plane, the humidity was something we had not remembered since we had been in Florida for almost two weeks. I have never been so glad to see St. Jude, but there was one catch. We could not get in the emergency door. As we stood outside in the summer heat with blankets on Trey, he began to become more conscious and uncomfortable. It was like being locked out of your own house, but you know someone is inside. So do you run around to the back or wait till they come to the door? You know, just as you would get to the back, the front door would open. We finally got in touch with someone from security to let us in and, since it was a weekend, it was just not normal for someone to come to that door.

When we got to the floor where Trey's room was located, it was good to see familiar nurses. They immediately began to get Trey comfortable and love on him. But I noticed something as Trey was rolled into the room. This was a very large room, corner room. Most of the rooms at St. Jude are lined down the hallway and are the size of a normal hospital room. The first thought I had was, "We are not going home."

Jay and the family left Panama City on Saturday at 6 p.m. and drove all night. They arrived in Memphis at 2:30 a.m. Sunday morning. Jay sent me a text when they got in. I was up feeding Trey his favorite, McAlister's potato soup. Since Trey slept most of Saturday, he was getting his time confused.

TREY: "Goodmorning princess :)" was the text from Trey to Julianne at 7:16 a.m. on Sunday. JULIANNE: "Goodmorning bubba :)" I know it does his heart good to know she is near.

We have tried to keep Trey comfortable. He has his pain pump for his pain medication, Dilaudid. They are giving him doses of Dilaudid on top of this and he receives a base rate. They increased several parts of these levels about three times today as his pain increased.

We dealt with Trey not being able to void today. This can be from several things. After discussing catheterizing him, I think one of the nurses actually scared the pee out of him. He felt much better and pain did subside a little around 4 p.m.

We have also had an issue with his blood pressure. At one point it was 159/105. He is being given large amounts of steroids; he is in pain; and he has a large amount of fluid, all of which can contribute to high blood pressure. They were starting him on a hypertension medication this evening to bring his blood pressure down until some of the fluid can be removed.

The doctors would like to go the medicine route first to see if the fluid can drain. We agree. The poking and draining doesn't fix anything! We don't know for certain that the fluid is malignant. Amazingly, ALL OF HIS BLOOD COUNTS ARE GOOD! Only his white count is up which could tell there is infection. They started him on albumin which draws the fluid out of the tissue. They then gave him lasix to flush the fluid out. Well, you can imagine all the fluid trying to pass and not being able to go. Trey just cannot get comfortable. He will sit up on the side of the bed and the lay back in the bed; back and forth.

From the beginning of the morning to the end of the afternoon, Trey's waist measured the same, but he gained a pound during the day. We can only assume this is fluid.

I talked to Dr. Sara tonight and things will be different tomorrow. We understand it is hard on the weekend at the hospital. Hopefully things will get rolling tomorrow and Trey will be on the road to feeling better. We know we have hurdles to overcome, but nothing is impossible. Remember Matthew 19:26? *"Jesus looked at them and said, with man this is impossible, but with God all things are possible."* And I can even say that about pain control! I'm claiming it in the small things, as well as the big things.

GOD IS STILL ON HIS THRONE; even with beeping machines, alarms going off, nurses running in, no sleep, and things unseen. As Trey's breathing changes, the alarms go off and I jump, but sometimes the nurses don't run in. That sometimes bothers me more. I know his stats are monitored at the desk but I'm still on the edge of my seat. Trey constantly wants to remove his oximeter off his finger. He can't understand why he needs his "ET phone home" light on his finger. Remember our ABC's - A is for Always having faith in our God, Doctors, Nurses, Family, Friends, and Ourselves!

CHAPTER 22

HOW DO THEY DO IT?

"Even though I walk through the valley of the shadow of death, I will fear no evil, for You are with me; Your rod and Your staff, they comfort me." Psalms 23:4

July 3, 2012

I have news to share. Honestly, I thought it would be coming much later than today. We met with the doctors yesterday. They read the scan from Florida and confirmed the cancer has spread to the areas mentioned in the report. As of now, our goal, Trey's goal, and the goal of all of the doctors is for Trey to make it to his birthday, July 31 – Trey Erwin Day, when he will turn 16. Medically, we have many things to be handled on an immediate basis; the first being the retention of his fluid. Even though they have started him on Lasix and other medications, it has not started to work fully (as it takes time to kick in). During this time, he gains more weight and fluid. We are hoping to have another solution for this by the end of the week. Trust me, I am all over this because of his pain. He can't move without being in pain and the drugs to remove the fluid aren't working fast enough.

Dr. Tauer came to see us today and helped us make many decisions. As we were talking, Trey asked if he could have some green tea. The nurse said we don't have any green tea up here.

"Maybe they have some in the cafeteria downstairs," answered Dr. Tauer.

"We'll go get some." And he got up and walked out of the room.

"Are you really going to go get him green tea?" I asked, following him out of the room.

"He said he wanted green tea," he replied, "and I'm going to go get him green tea."

I just smiled as it gave us time to walk to the cafeteria and talk. I told him I knew Trey wanted to go home, but I just didn't think we could handle Trey at home. By the time we had made it back to the room, Dr. Tauer's arm was around my shoulder. He told me what a great job we were doing and what a fine son we had raised. That's quite a high compliment coming from a Christian physician who cares so deeply for his patients. He told me we would know what was right when the time comes. I so want to hold to Trey's wishes, but in my mind, I know God's plan. We never found any green tea but I let Dr. Tauer break that news to Trey. I know God anointed our time together.

Trey said his first goal was to get home. Dr. Tauer, Dr. Sara, and Karen Williams, feel it's very important for Trey have a say in his care. If, at any time, we feel Trey needs to come back to St. Jude, the doors are wide open. Being at home will make him feel better and he will have a chance to get his room organized. Our plans are to go home with a hospital bed. We don't think Trey will be comfortable in his bed like HE thinks he will. As Dr. Tauer suggested, we are going to clean out the dining room so he can bed hop and get to any place he's comfortable. Our first thought was how much our two labs are going to love hopping in the hospital bed with Trey.

After we met with the doctors, Trey and I were alone in his room.

"Mom," he asked. "Can I write a Will?"

I answered, "Sure buddy. Just put it in the Notes section of your phone and we will do whatever you want. Do you want me to type it in for you?"

"No, I'll do it," he responded. He put his phone down on his chest.

Nothing else was ever mentioned on the subject. I knew it would be hard for him to type on his phone. He has had many text messages from friends. I know he tried to read them, but he has not been able to respond because of the pain or his vision. Maybe, he just does not know what to say at this point.

So many people have told us they don't know how we do it. We've been called an inspiration. Trey's been called an inspiration. We feel like others have been the inspiration for us. We have such a special relationship with Dr. Sara Federico. Some days, I don't know what I would have done without her. There is no way to describe the special measures she goes to for her patients. Dr. Tauer, Dr. Sara, Karen William are a few of the many people that have helped us down this difficult road. Their caring spirits and the evidence of their own faith has been so helpful. God knew the doctors Trey would need. HE KNEW the support Jay and I would need in this crisis of not understanding the full picture and he gave us men and women who love and trust in Him.

We have always trusted God to guide our every step. Maybe we have missed some doors that closed during the journey, but, because we have held fast to our faith, we have not recognized the doors as being closed. They have just allowed us to see other avenues as opportunities. He has been faithful in leading us down each path. God knows our hurts and our fears. We are hurting and I would be lying if I said we were not afraid. We are His creatures and He tells us in His word to lean on Him.

We ask for your prayers for all of us. Pray for our precious Collin, who will turn 13 on July 20. Trey loves him very much and this will be a hard thing for Collin to experience in the coming month and years. During this journey, Trey has wanted to talk to Collin so many times. They have spent countless hours together watching movies, playing video games, and just taking naps. But I don't think Trey has had the opportunity to tell Collin exactly how he feels. Trey has told me how much he loves Collin, but there is just something about hearing it from the person you love, brother to brother.

So, this is how we do it. I opened just now my phone to search God's word to leave you with scripture and this is the verse of the day. *"I believe that the present suffering is nothing compared to the coming glory that is going to be revealed to us." Romans 8:18*

July 4, 2012

It pains me to know there are celebrations going on all over the city while I watch Trey gasp each time he moves. We ask for your prayers for Trey at this time as he battles extreme pain. We also know July 31 is looking unrealistic as things are progressing very fast.

He is scheduled to have fluid removed tomorrow. It's possible he will have another block also. Please pray for guidance for the doctors and for a peaceful night for Trey. His nausea and pain are winning. He has started to talk about some weird things. I have to ask myself, are the drugs really getting to him or is it something else?

"Mom," Collin commented, "it looks like the cancer has gotten ahead of us." Never underestimate the mind of a 12 year old.

Pam, the nurse who was his date to walk around the hallway, is with us this July 4th. She asked if he wanted to go down to the sitting area where everyone was gathered to watch the fireworks. Trey said no. Instead, she brought us all glow in the dark bracelets and Jay, Trey and I wore them to celebrate Independence Day.

He is still able to get up to go to the bathroom. Sometimes it's even a comfortable place for him to just sit for a moment. He leans back against pillows to relieve the pressure on his abdomen. If he is not in the bathroom, he will just sit up in bed and I will let his back lean against my shoulder and my side as if he is stretching. If it makes him feel better, we will try it.

Trey was still holding his phone. It was going off constantly with texts from people I had never heard of. Unfortunately, he was not able to answer. At 3:16 this afternoon, I sent him a text:

LISA: "I love you thiissss much!"

That has always been what we would tell each other since he was a little boy. He didn't respond. That would be the last text he would ever read.

He is resting a little more comfortably. He is still in pain, but it seems they have reached a level of medication that is helping him. We have, actually, been pushing the pain pump for him. Around 8 p.m. tonight, he became unresponsive, so I know he was not in pain. I am still jumping as his monitors go off, so they have disconnected the monitor in the room. We can still see his oxygen levels, his blood pressure, and his heart rate. It just does not send me over the edge when he is only breathing 10 times a minute.

CHAPTER 23

10,000 REASONS

*"Therefore, if anyone is in Christ, he is a new creation; the old
has gone, the new has come!"*
2 Corinthians 5:17

July 5, 2012

Dr. Sara came in very early and told us, according to Trey's labs, everything is shutting down. He has not had any urine output in over 24 hours, so his kidneys have stopped functioning. Even though Trey has evidence of some oral secretions, we requested he not be suctioned, if possible. They were so gentle with him and were actually administering medication so there were no signs of distress. He only aroused once to ask for Benadryl, but he fell into a deep, deep sleep very quickly afterwards.

Tara and Corbin Peeper came by around 10 a.m. to see us. They were on their way to Florida for their family vacation and wanted to stop by before they left. I was so glad they did. About that time, Trey made a movement like he was going to throw up. Jay and I ran to him and sat him up on the side of the bed. He had no control over his muscles and dark green bile ran out of the side of his mouth. I cleaned him up and we laid him back in bed. Tara and Corbin left and I asked if they would please give Jim a big hug for all of us.

Around 11:30 a.m., Dr. Sara came in and told us she didn't think Trey had much longer. People started gathering in the room. When I told the nurses I wanted to get in the bed with Trey, they picked up the corners of the sheets and moved him to one side. When they did he groaned.

"Trey," I asked. "If you can hear me, squeeze my hand buddy." There was no response. Because of his reaction to being moved, I knew he was still with me in some way.

News was spreading to Collierville and his friends were coming by. Isaiah Downey, Eli Willard, and Brantley Green came by as I was in the bed with Trey. I told Isaiah Trey could hear him and he was free to talk to him. I saw the pain in Isaiah's face, but I knew he needed to get it out.

"I love you Trey," he said. "You'll always be my brother and I'll always be here for Collin." I hugged Isaiah and watched him walk to the back of the room with his fellow teammates.

Ryan Mullins came in and leaned against the window seat. Cindy Few was at my head, playing with my hair as I talked to Trey. I began to remind Trey of all of our vacations together. I walked down memory lane with him of our train vacation to Montana and how he considered that a "real vacation" as we traveled through Chicago across the country to Glacier National Park. I talked about all our Florida vacations and Collierville football games. I reminded him of the fun we had in Hawaii and what he considered his paradise. I told him of the paradise he was about to see would not compare to Hawaii.

I sang the song that I sang to him as a baby over and over.
"You are my sunshine,
my only sunshine.
You make me happy,
when times are grey.
You'll never know dear,
how much I love you.
Please don't take my sunshine away."

I asked for my phone and began to whisper scripture that he had tweeted in his ear. Collin had been sitting in the chair next to Ryan. I gently pulled him in the bed with me and laid him on top of me where he would not be facing Trey for his own protection. It would be his choice to roll over. During this time, Ryan was playing music from Hillsong, music we sang at camp, music from Passion, and other worship songs. People continued to gather in the room. At one point, as "White Flag" by Chris Tomlin was playing, I looked up and saw Dr. Sara on the other side of Trey singing, with her eyes closed and her head lifted up. Standing next to her was Jay with Cojo (Courtney Jordan), Karson Jones, Madison Young and Julianne surrounding him. Tim Few was at Trey's feet. At that moment, I realized people were worshipping and I could not help but cry as I scanned the room filled with over 20 plus people.

Jay was able to whisper to me his breathing had changed and we knew it would not be long. Our pastors, Charles Fowler, Keith Cochran, Ron Norton, and Allen Jones, were with us along with many friends and family. During this time, Ryan leaned over to me and whispered he had a word from God and he didn't think it would be long. I was puzzled. How did he know this?

Trey's breathing began to slow. My prayer had always been that Trey wouldn't die at night. I have a fear of night and, I knew, if Trey died at night, it would make my grieving so much worse. His breathing went from 10 breaths a minute to much slower, but it was not labored. I kept stroking his face and his hair while singing in his ear.

Julianne looked at Ryan and told him to play "10,000 Reasons". The song began to play and the room began to sing.
"And on that day when my strength is failing,
The end draws near and my time has come..."
On the last verse, Trey took his last breath.

"Run to Jesus buddy. Run to Jesus as hard as you can," I said as I continued to stroke his silky eyebrows.

I heard my sister, Donna, scream in tears. Tim collapsed on the bed at Trey's feet sobbing. Jay picked up a stethoscope.

"What are you doing?" I asked.

I think he needed to hear for himself. Dr. Sara took the stethoscope from Jay and listened also. Then, she kissed Trey's head and told him to go be with Jesus. I looked up at her and heard the question "Is this really happening?" go through my head.

At 3:30 p.m. I posted *"Trey is now healthy in heaven."* Ryan stopped the music and the room began to clear. I could not move out of the bed, not just yet. I saw Julianne collapse in her daddy's arms as they both cried.

I asked Ron Norton, "Why do I feel so guilty about having a peace?"

"Why should you feel guilty," he answered, "when so many are praying for you?"

Bretta Cochran and the nurses helped clear the room so we could tend to Trey. I had no idea there were others that had been in the waiting area the entire time. Julianne stayed with Jay and me. I could not get Trey's bracelets off, so Julianne and I had a couple of laughs trying to get them off his wrists. I also asked for a pair of scissors and a baggie.

I looked at Julianne and said, "He would kill me if he knew I was doing this." Then, I cut a lock of hair off the back of his head to put in my wallet.

> **Julianne Shiles' Thoughts:** When I lost Trey, I thought it wasn't real and he was going to come back. I miss being able to text him and talk to him. Trey was always there

for me. I lost my best friend and the love of my life. He taught me what it meant to completely trust in God with no worries. I'll take that with me the rest of my life. Hakuna Matata.

Julianne kissed us goodbye. We had final questions to handle with Dr. Sara and Karen Williams. Honestly, they were questions I was not prepared for and had not discussed with Trey. Did he want to be an organ donor? It hit me like a ton of bricks as if I was offended, but I wasn't. I thought, "My baby just died and I have to answer this?" Dr. Sara and Karen were so sweet to tell us it was all procedure that they have to ask and I just kept looking at Trey telling them "No, no, no."

As we packed his bags and belongings, I turned and looked at Trey lying in the bed. I knew it was not really Trey, but turning and walking out of the room at St. Jude was the hardest thing I have ever done. I was leaving a part of me in that bed; a large part of me that would never come home again.

July 11, 2012

"What do we do now?" I asked when Jay and I got in the car.

"I don't know," he said. "Go home, I guess."

When we arrived home, media trucks from every local station lined our street and our yard was full of friends and family with candles lit for Trey. People were coming in and out of our house and my mind was blank. I knew plans needed to be made soon.

When Tara Peeper walked in, I said, "I thought you were in Florida!"

When they heard of Trey's turn, they cancelled their trip and stayed in town. I was so glad because I wanted Corbin to be a pallbearer.

Keith Cochran, Ryan Mullins, and I escaped to the playroom to begin making preparations for Trey's celebration. Before he died, Trey made it clear it was to be a celebration, not a funeral. The days after his passing were a blessing from God. We were so blessed by so many friends. We were able to plan his celebration without a hitch, mostly because we knew Trey's wishes. And what a celebration it was! I think Trey probably had his shades on enjoying some Beach Boys too!

We made sure the word got out for everyone to wear pastel or bright shirts. Cojo, Karson, and Julianne went on a run around the city for glow sticks like Trey wanted. Gathering Trey's clothes to take to the funeral home took all of 10 minutes. He needed a Polo shirt, Polo bowtie, Polo pants, Polo socks, and Polo shoes. I found out, when the St. Jude staff came in to take Trey from his room, one of his nurses, Judy, made sure they didn't mess up his hair. I am sure Trey appreciated that, from heaven. I find it humorous! Nothing should mess up the Beiber hair, what chemotherapy had left of it. What great love and respect they had for Trey.

Keith and Ryan went with us to the funeral home to make plans with Memorial Park. We even laughed then and it relieved so much of the tension in the air. Ryan had walked through a similar situation of losing a young person at his church, so he was able to be a very big help in telling us what to expect with the funeral home. Memorial Park blessed us.

Saturday, July 7, I got up and got ready like I was getting ready for church. But it was no ordinary service. I had not been to a funeral service with over 3,000 people. We had requested the media remain off the grounds of the church. The Memphis Fire Department had fire trucks on the property in front of the church in memory of Trey.

Having a service in a church is so very different than a funeral home. We we were to have private time before the service, but it just was not as private as I would have wished. There are many things parents desire as "special touches".

It was Jay's desire to close Trey's casket and he did. He removed Trey's class ring, his favorite purple polo bow tie from around his neck, and closed the lid. I am thankful I was in the parlor of our church with the family at the time before the service.

> **Coach Mike O'Neill's Thoughts:** I have never felt the power of the HOLY SPIRT as strong I did than at Trey's funeral. I, honestly, was almost overwhelmed with emotion when it was my turn to speak. However, as I walked to the podium, I knew I wasn't alone. The presence of GOD was so strong and I knew TREY ERWIN was in that church! I could not let them down.

It was good to have D. J. Stephens and his fiancée, Stacie Payne, with the rest of the family during the celebration. As Trey and I had discussed, Anna Wakefield sang "Your Great Name". We sang others he had requested: "10,000 Reasons", "Forever Reign", and "The Stand". I held on to every word not wanting the service to end. During the last song, I looked over at Trey's pallbearers and they were singing without smiles when we were belting "I Lay Me Down".

I was hopping all over the place knowing that was what Trey was doing. So I bolted across the aisle and stood in between the guys with my arms wrapped around them and they beamed. I wanted them to know their friend was still with them in their heart.

We made every Germantown Baptist student an honorary pallbearer, along with the pallbearers he would have wanted: Tim Few, Corbin Peeper, Daniel Roberts, Taylor Morse, Jimmy Gresham, Cody Jordan, Hunter Byer, and Bobby Thorne.

Trey was a fan of the Beach Boys and we knew he would want them played at his celebration. As Trey was taken out of the church, the Beach Boys played. We heard laughter and saw smiles as we walked down the aisle. We requested the Collierville High School football team line the foyer. As we drove down Poplar Avenue to Memorial Park, we watched as cars pulled to the side and people get out of their cars.

The graveside service was very brief and we didn't linger. Trey's casket was covered with words of love written by friends and family. A gentle rain began to fall and we headed back to the church. We had food for friends and family at the church, so we returned to eat, as most Baptists do well.

As the rain continued to fall, Cojo and Karson grabbed Jay and said, "Mr. Jay, come on, let's go dance in the rain." In the spirit of celebrating Trey's life, Jay did exactly what he should have done.

"Sure, let's do it!" he said.

And while the sun was shining and the rain continued to come down a hot, July day, Jay and Trey's friends danced in the rain to celebrate a boy who lived his life to the fullest, checked off his bucket list, put others before himself, and, most of all, brought glory to God, even in death.

"And I saw the holy city, new Jerusalem, coming down out of heaven from God, made ready as a bride adorned for her husband. And I heard a loud voice from the throne, saying, "Behold, the tabernacle of God is among men, and He will dwell among them, and they shall be His people, and God Himself will be among them, and He will wipe away every tear from their eyes; and there will no longer be any death; there will no longer be any mourning, or crying, or pain; the first things have passed away.""" Revelation 21: 2-4

CHAPTER 24

THE NEW NORMAL

"So then, just as you received Christ Jesus as Lord, continue to live your lives in him, rooted and built up in him, strengthened in the faith as you were taught, and overflowing with thankfulness."
Colossians 2:6, 7

Grief is an oddity. I think of it like Highway 385 in Collierville, Tennessee. It is a highway we cannot avoid if we want to get anywhere in the vicinity of Collierville. There are many exits and we have the choice to hop off at any given time. Grief has many components - tears, anger, depression, sadness, guilt, loneliness, anxiety, and many other stages. Our family is traveling the highway at different speeds since Trey has passed. We have all hopped off different exits without being able to reach each other by phone, so to speak. We may camp out for a while and hop back on the highway and travel a little further down the road a hop off another exit, such as loneliness or sadness. The point is, we are all at different stages and we will continue on that highway for a long time. We are not moving on, we are just moving along the highway not knowing when it will end.

We have tangible things to we hold on to. St. Jude had pillows that were very small and moldable. Jay and I sleep with one pillow, used to support Trey's during those last days and hours between us. We never speak about the pillow between us. It represents our sweet boy and all he went through. Many nights, I cry into that pillow.

Just after Trey died, I had several people give me well-meaning advice. One person told me, "You just need to learn to love God more than you do Trey." I have never hurt so much and I was so offended. I wanted to scream, "My son just died, you have your healthy children, and you want to talk to ME about loving GOD?" It took a while before what she said actually made sense. That has now become my desire. As much as I want to be with Trey in heaven, my ultimate desire is to be at the feet of Jesus to worship Him WITH my son. It is all a part of the grief process. I don't love God any less than I did three years ago. As a matter of fact, I know I love Him more for the wonderful gift He gave us in Trey. I have said many times to friends, I don't cry during worship because I miss Trey. I cry because I am so thankful for Christ dying on the cross for our sins. If He would not have died so sacrificially, MY son would not be in heaven. What a gift from God.

So many wonderful tributes happened after Trey's passing. We knew it would be hard attending the Collierville football games, but Collierville is family and they welcomed us and loved us during both seasons. During the first season, Coach O'Neill (Mike) and the coaching staff chose a player each week to wear #13 based upon their hard work on the field and in the classroom. It was exciting to see each week who they would select.

> **Coach Mike O'Neill's Thoughts:** Trey's faith and strength was an inspiration to our football team during those months leading up to his death and during the season. I remember Trey was on the sideline during the maroon/white game that May, a couple of months before his death, and the disease really was taking a toll on his body. That was a time that the majority of his teammates could observe the magnitude of his condition. I believe most of his teammates knew it

would be his last game. Players wanted to incorporate summer training with team runs over to Trey's house for visits and be closer to their brother. That year, my first year as a head coach, our team built a foundation of working hard for each other, doing the best with what God gave us and never complaining. In that time, each player understood how precious his time on earth is and the importance of individual faith. We dedicated that season to Trey and rotated his number #13 to the player the coaching staff voted that week for the effort and determination that individual gave in preparation for that game. The competition to wear #13 was fierce! "PLAY FOR TREY" was our chant and the 4th quarter was the time to leave it on the field. It was known as "Trey's Quarter."

We felt it was only right to give back to the school that had given us so much. They were able to renovate the visitor's box and chose to paint on the box "And There Was in the Land a Mighty Dragon" Erwin 13. I had the opportunity to visit the field just after the box was completed. I walked to the middle of the field and sat down on the fresh cut grass. Trey considered the field his holy ground on earth. I heaved as tears rolled down my face uncontrollably. Trey probably would not have wanted it, but it was such an honor. One day it will be painted over again with another color and different writing. But for now, it honors a boy who loved his Dragon family.

During the same season, Coach O'Neill (Mike) surprised us by having the hospital Wing land in the middle of the field and deliver the game ball to us signed by all the players. He usually does not get much by me, but he pulled this surprise off!

The 2013-14 football season was Trey's senior year. Mike decided to wait until senior night to have the number #13 worn. It was worn by Corbin Peeper, one of Trey's pallbearers. Jay and I bought all the seniors yellow roses to give to them as they were announced and walked out to hug their mothers. I didn't know they each had a pink rose for me. They took their yellow roses and left them on the #13 painted at the goal line of the field during a moment of silence and prayed before the game. You could hear a pin drop in the Collierville stands.

Later that evening, I was still on the field after the game and Jay had walked up the hill. Everyone was gone except the coaching staff. I was standing with Tara, Corbin's mother, and we were having a moment between us, as we often do. I turned and took a quick glance at the scoreboard. The game clock had stopped on 13 seconds. I collapsed in Tara's arms and Mike ran to me wanting to know what was wrong. I asked if that had been done on purpose. The clock operators were there and said, "No, No." They immediately turned the scoreboard off. Little things, such as this, make me wonder if God gives us signs that Trey is still with us. Well, it scared me to death.

During the summer before the season started, Mike began running an idea by Jay and me about an award he wanted to start during the 2013-14 season. We told him we had already planned to begin a Trey Erwin Memorial Football Scholarship in the amount of $1,300. The first year the scholarship was awarded to Mitch Owens. Each person read all the scholarship applications kept coming back to the same application, Mitch Owens. It was an easy pick.

Mike had a more difficult task with what ultimately became the Erwin Award. This award is voted on by the football peers, much like the Heisman. The inaugural Erwin Award went to Corbin Peeper. The large trophy with a plate on the award stays at the school and Corbin was able to take a smaller award home. The award and scholarship was presented at the football banquet on November 12, 2013. In return, I received a banner with Trey's name, number, and position (wide receiver) commemorating his senior year, just as every player received. It was a special evening for the entire team.

Corbin Peepers' Thoughts: If you were to look down the sidelines at any time, you would see Trey and I next to one another. Trey was more than the average teammate or schoolmate, his humble and humorous presence was something everyone could enjoy. Trey and I grew up playing sports together; basketball at church when we were little to young men in a football uniform. Very few times did I ever see Trey down and those occasions were because he didn't reach a personal goal or a challenge between us in the weight room. Trey and I spent countless hours together competing and pushing each other to greater levels of strength and conditioning. Trey and I had a goal to reach 175 pounds before our junior football season. Trey was having trouble putting on weight and I remember this frustrating him greatly. Trey never complained, even when he, unknowingly, had cancer and continued to train seldomly saying anything to me about pains in his stomach. After he was diagnosed, I saw the Trey I saw everyday. He never complained, but instead embraced the pains and trusted God with his life and where he was going. Trey's influence on me will last a lifetime, an eternal lifetime. Every time I am feeling defeated or discouraged, I remember that God has a plan and that what is important is I trust Him in all circumstances. Trey didn't worry about his future because he knew ultimately what it would be, eternal life with his Father, he just asked "that His will be done". Trey spread the word of God to countless people he had never met and brought a broken and failing team together as a family. Trey walks with me everyday and continues to fuel my walk with Christ. Trey was a blessing to my life and will never be forgotten. I am honored to be the first recipient of the Erwin Award and I KNOW Trey, my friend, would be proud. But I don't think he would ever let me live down that I reached 175 pounds first.

We have celebrated Trey in ways other than football. One thing on his bucket list he was not able to check off was his 16th birthday. School and church friends gathered at Germantown Baptist and we released balloons in his memory. For some reason, the sky was cloudy that day. We also celebrated his 17th birthday on the Collierville football field with purple balloons flashing in the dark. Friends and family were in the stands and on the count of three, balloons flew into the night sky like purple lightening bugs. I stood in the middle of the football field with Andy

Shiles, Julianne's dad, and we shed tears together as he remarked he had lost a son too. The Shiles family, like many other families and friends, are grieving alongside us.

We have only had one anniversary and we spent it with Trey's friends. I had just returned from taking "his girls" on a cruise for their senior trip (Julianne Shiles, Madison Young, Leighton Newman, and Katie Beth Hopkins). We spent the week laughing and talking about Trey, so it alleviated some of the stress of coming home to July 5, the day we flew back. That evening, we watched "The Lion King" and knew he would have been right there in the middle of us as everyone sang Hakuna Matata.

Aside from all the highlight activities over the last year and a half, we have tried to function as a family of three instead a family of four. When Jay goes to work, it is just Collin, me and the dogs. It is hard to cook for just two, so fast food is our friend. I realize the things that were so important before, are not so important anymore. I catch myself laughing at others trying to make difficult decisions when, in the big scheme of life, if you have God by your side, everything can be so much easier.

But here is the catch. I have realized through Trey's journey and after his death, the only way we survived is because of God's amazing grace and His strength. It is still a daily struggle. I have said many times I want my boy back. I have screamed, begged, and cried, sometimes sliding down the bathroom wall just like he did.

> *"He has made everything beautiful in its time.*
> *He has also set eternity in the hearts of men;*
> *yet they cannot fathom what God has done*
> *from beginning to end." Ecclesiastes 3:11*

My faith holds to this scripture Trey would not want to come back to us. It's true we cannot understand what God began in Trey's life, but God's plans are perfect and Trey fulfilled God's plan for his life of 15 years. I always tell people two things when they ask me how hold to our faith:

1. God can redeem anything for good.
2. He always has a perfect plan.

Collin is now a St. Jude patient because he also carries the P16 gene. Trey didn't know before he died. We are still blessed to have Dr. Sara in our life as Collin's doctor. Collin will continue to be screened without radiation. They are watching his pancreas, blood work, and all other areas the P16 gene affects. We pray continually he will remain clear of any cancer and grow to be a man of God with his own testimony.

I cannot hear Trey's voice as loud as I did a year ago. And, when the garage door opens, I don't jump thinking he'll walk in the door calling "Mom, I'm home." I don't see his face in every teenage boy. Many say the first year is the hardest. I was just numb!

The second year is when reality set that he's gone. I have actually had to tell people my son is dead. People are moving on with their life, but Trey's clothes still hang in his closet. I see people many places such as the checkout line at WalMart, Kroger, restaurants, and they will say, "I know you from somewhere."

I simply tell them, "I am Trey Erwin's mother." That is when their light bulb goes off. It does not embarrass me as much as it does them. I'm proud to have been his mom and I know Jay is just as proud to have been his dad.

If there is one thing this journey taught us as parents, it is to stick to our discipline family rules no matter what the popular thing is to do. We didn't let Trey hang out at the movie theater in 6th grade; we limited his activities with school friends; and ended relationships when we believed they were not in his best interest. Of course, Trey thought

THEN he was dying. Maybe, just maybe, our discipline was for the greater good in his journey.

We must face the fact we will all face death and will all meet our Savior. I tried my best to instill in Trey whatever you do, do all for the glory of God. I believe he met that goal. But is that your goal? There are many avenues to meet that goal each day, i.e. prayer, bible study, Godly choices, worship, service to others, and the list goes on. When I wake up each morning, these are my goals.

> *"For the grace of God has appeared, bringing salvation to all men, instructing us to deny ungodliness and worldly desires and to live sensibly, righteously and godly in the present age." Titus 2:12*

I don't think there will be a day a switch will flip and the agonizing pain of the loss of Trey will suddenly have disappeared. But I do know each day God is faithful to fulfill our needs as a family and He continues to grow us into the unit we need to be. Even through all the pain, there is still peace. A calming peace that I know when I go to meet Jesus, my son will be with Jesus to meet me.

My first words will be, "I love you thiisssss much!"

Obituary of Jerry Wayne Erwin, III

July 5, 2012

Jerry Wayne "Trey" Erwin, III, of Collierville, TN passed away on July 5, 2012, just a few weeks shy of his 16th birthday. Trey attended Collierville High School where he had completed his Sophomore year and played Receiver on the Collierville Dragon Football Team. He started playing football at the age of 5. He was a very active member of Germantown Baptist Church, serving in the Germantown Student Ministry and Under Authority Youth Choir. He served in Children's Worship and went on many mission trips. Trey was diagnosed with pancreatic cancer on March 6th and his first remarks were - "I'll be okay", "I'll either be healthy here, or healthy in Heaven". Since Trey was diagnosed, God gave him a platform for the last four months of his life to declare that Jesus is in control and that he is going to be okay. That peace spread throughout the nation via a campaign on Twitter labeled #prayfortrey. The family would like to express their deepest appreciation to all of the Collierville Community for all of their support, as well as the thousands more from around the Nation. Trey is survived by his parents, Jerry "Jay" Erwin Jr., and Lisa C. Erwin; his brother, Collin Erwin; his grandmothers, Cecelia Erwin and Lena E. Hutcherson; uncle, Terry Erwin; aunts, Judy Riley and Donna Thorne (Bill); many other extended family members; and a "Host of Dragons". He was preceded in death by his grandfathers, Leonard M. Hutcherson, Jerry W. Erwin, Sr.; his great-grandmother, Hazel Caldwell "Lil Grandma"; and his uncle, Barry Erwin.

CONCLUSION

By Reverend Keith W. Cochran

STANDING IN THE SHADOW

There are certain things you are just simply not prepared for. When I was a Student Pastor, I was supposed to be prepared for anything and everything. When we went to camp, I generally prepared for rainy days and roadside emergencies. On a mission trip I might plan for additional service projects, an extra worship service, or a movie night in the event of a sudden change of plans. In the office, you never know what that next phone call, counseling appointment, or email might bring your way. But nothing prepares you for what we went through with the Erwin family. Nothing prepares you, yet we are more than adequately prepared.

Paul tells us about this in 2 Corinthians. Paul was asking for a trial to be removed. Instead of removing it, God reminded Paul of His presence. 2 Corinthians 12:9 says, *"and He has said to me, 'My grace is sufficient for you, for power is perfected in weakness.' Most gladly, therefore, I will rather boast about my weaknesses, so that the power of Christ may dwell in me."* Did you see that? Paul definitely did not want to know what we can or cannot handle. But at best, we want to handle it. And when we cannot handle it, what then? God's power is perfected in our weakness. God's power shows up and reminds us that He was there strengthening us all along. His strength not our strength. His. When we feel weakest, God is there. He is not there to point out our weakness. He is not there to challenge why we are weakest. He is there showing His power, perfecting in us His presence. We are carried by

~263~

His strength. We are sustained by His strength. We are supported by His very presence.

I have one question: where do you stand when you face trials? There are all sorts of trials and struggles that people walk through. Some are life and death diagnoses involving you or a loved one. Some people deal with a job crisis. Some struggle with a test result, financial hardship, loss of relationship, abuse, neglect, ongoing illness, and much more. We each have a place to stand in the midst of these struggles. We can either stand in the shadow of the problem, or we can walk in the shadow of the cross.

When you walk in the shadow of the problem, you get overwhelmed. Your vision is impaired because you are in the shadows. In Psalm 23 David proclaims, *"even though I walk through the valley of the shadow of death, I will fear no evil. For You are with me."* There is that shadow. The shadow of death. How in the world can anyone walk through this valley and not fear evil and death? Is it even possible?

I know it is possible. I watched a fifteen year-old teenage boy walk through that valley. How did he do it? Here's the best news: He did not walk alone. You see, the rest of that passage in Psalm 23 is the key. "You are with me." There is the promise. God walks with us through these times.

Let me fill you in on Trey. He was definitely not the perfect kid. He was a teenager. He had struggles. He had frustrations. Sometimes he was a carrier of them! Sometimes he acted like a teenage boy who struggled with girls and friends and family and grades and pride and sin. In other words, he was like each of us - imperfect. To learn a little about Trey, let me share with you a couple of fun stories that I shared at his funeral.

I remember a trip to Westwego, LA. We went there for a mission trip. It was hot. It was difficult. Trey worked so hard. He kept up with the "big kids", even thought he was younger than most of the guys on the trip. This was in 2008, so I think Trey was finishing 7th grade. There was a time when all the guys got together for a picture. Well, posing for a picture with a group of teenage boys is like trying to get cats and dogs to pose together. Inevitably a wrestling match broke out. After we broke up the scrum, Trey came back to me and asked if I was ok. I thought he was checking to make sure that 15 guys piling on his beloved youth pastor didn't hurt, injure, or maim me. I told him, "sure, I'm fine" (I probably wasn't fine, but I wasn't going to tell a 7th grader that a teenage dog pile was too much...). He smiled and replied, "I wanted to make sure I didn't hurt you". He had no shortage of confidence.

I also learned that one year at Disciple Now he and his group played one of those video game sing-a-long games. He sang to a perfect score...of Hannah Montana music. Again, he had no shortage of confidence.

Then about a year before his cancer, during spring football practice, Trey came walking down the hall of Germantown Baptist Church coming to our Wednesday night student service. He was with his good friend Hunter. They were a little late since they were coming straight from football. There was only one problem...Trey had no shirt on. I said "Trey, what are you doing? Why don't you have a shirt on?" He looked at me, and then pointed to his skinny physique, and said, "would you cover this up?" He did eventually put a shirt on before heading into the service that night. He really had no shortage of confidence.

But then, when his life was literally on the line, when he first heard his diagnosis, Trey's response showed his confidence, and the source of that confidence. We are sitting in St. Jude. The doctors are telling him that he has a rare form of cancer, and that his life expectancy is short. All of a sudden he cracks this smile and says these words: "I'll be ok. I'll be healed here, or I'll be healed in heaven". What?!?! How does he say that? Why does he say that? I'm sure he later prays asking God to take away this extreme "thorn in the flesh". But not right then. He was just told he might not live to see 16. How does a teenager respond that way? He responds that way when, in his weakness, God's strength is being perfected in his life at that very moment. He responds that way when he knows where he is standing. Trey was not going to stand in the shadow of cancer. Nope. He held out hope of healing on earth, but knew he was going to be healed one way or the other.

This is not just some kid hoping, thinking positive, or having a strong outlook. This was a young man who really did listen to his parents (although sometimes they were not really sure if he was). This was a young man who loved Jesus, loved to worship Him, and had no shortage of confidence because His faith was in Jesus. He had surrendered. He had surrendered His life to Jesus. He was at peace because he lived in the shadow. He did not live in the shadow of cancer, but he lived in the shadow of the cross.

Trey and I had several conversations over the next several months. He still struggled knowing he was dying of cancer. Please do not think that Trey just skipped through the last few months of his life looking forward to death. Trey was uncomfortable with it. He was uncomfortable with leaving his family and his friends. He was very uncomfortable with the media attention and "popularity" that was coming his way. He and I talked about his platform. He had a platform to point people to Jesus. He had a platform that he could use for God's glory.

How do you walk in the shadow of the cross? Surrender. Surrender to Jesus. Romans 10:9 begins with *"If we confess with our mouth, Jesus is Lord...:"* This does not mean we make Jesus Lord. He is already Lord. But we must each surrender to Him as Lord. When I live a life surrendered to Jesus as Lord, I tend to walk in the shadow of the cross. This means I live each day letting the cross of Christ influence me and my daily life.

There are days when we struggle. The Erwin's will tell you, there are days that they struggle to walk in the shadow of the cross. There are days I struggle. Usually we struggle because somewhere along the way we get our focus on us and off the cross. When that happens, I tend to walk away from that shadow. Walking away from that shadow means I start to react and act in my sinful nature. I say and do things that simply do not honor God. But there is always room to walk in the shadow of the cross again. I turn from that sinful attitude and action and let Jesus cleanse me.

Sometimes we think that the work of the cross was accomplished 2000 years ago, and then somehow that work stopped. We get in our heads that we need to add into our lives where the cross leaves off. This shows two problems in our theology. First of all, the cross cannot be added to. There is no action, work, feeling, ritual, experience, or anything devised by man that can add to the cross. The cross was enough! The second problem is that the cross never leaves off. John MacArthur says, "the cross keeps moving powerfully and relentlessly through history, and it will stand forever as living proof that men cannot redeem themselves."

Jay, Lisa, and Collin cannot live their lives standing in the shadow of cancer, sickness, depression, heartache, Trey, or anything else that comes their way. Neither can we. We cannot stand in the shadow of a diagnosis, job struggle, crisis, or any other issue or problem. But we cannot stand in the shadow of the positive either. Sometimes we want to linger in the shadow of a promotion, good experience, pay raise, relational encouragement, health, and more. When we stand in either of these shadows, our focus turns to the thing that is causing the shadow. But when we walk in the shadow of the cross, we are focused on the work of Jesus, and the Light of the world that is casting that shadow. It is then that we can say *"...for You are with me. Your rod and your staff they comfort me. You prepare a table before me in the presence of my enemies. You anoint my head with oil. My cup runs over."* (Psalm 23:4b-5)

ACKNOWLEDGMENTS

How do I thank everyone that did so much for our family in such a short span of time? It's just impossible to do. There were times that Jay and I came home and people had been there and we did not know it. Unfortunately, there is someone I will leave out and I apologize.

St. Jude Children's Research Hospital is the top children's hospital in the world. God gave us Dr. Sara Federico, Dr. Alberto Pappo, Dr. Justin Baker, Karen Williams, and all the floor nurses. I know you did the best you could to give Trey the best quality of life. I am still amazed how God weaves people together for His glory. We made a great team and I am thankful we remain a team with Collin.

West Clinic, you add to the amazing team at St. Jude. Dr. Kurt Tauer, Dr. Tom Hodgkiss, Dr. Scott Baum, Neal Davis, Duston Williamson, and all the nurses that administered Trey's chemotherapy and took care of him after each procedure. He never dreaded going to West Clinic because he knew he would receive the best care and would feel better. You are all amazing people.

My beloved Pastor, Dr. Charles A. Fowler. You have been our Pastor, counselor, and friend. We are blessed that you were all of those to Trey also. He cherished your friendship and he loved you. He trusted your advice so much to call you in his final hours. We will never be able to repay the number of hours you have prayed for our family.

The single most influence on earth, outside of Jay and I was Reverend Keith Cochran, Pastor of West Jackson Baptist Church, Tupelo, Mississippi. There may be many visions that have been lost to memory, but the two of you together is forever etched in my mind. You and Bretta will forever be our 2 a.m. friends. You certainly were during our journey with Trey, and before! Thank you for teaching Trey how to put God first in his life. We've travelled on many bus trips and been on countless camps. I have seen you tired, recovering from knee surgery, with migraines, but you never wavered from your service of the Lord. I'll forever hold close to my heart Trey's last devotion he wrote on June 29 because he used action points. And you taught him Action Points!

Reverend Ryan Mullins, you and Anne stole Trey's heart in 6th grade and helped him develop his goofiness. I credit you with messy days, chocolate beards, and lots of love and laughter. For Jay and me, if only people could have been a fly on the wall with us in the funeral home together with Keith. Not many can turn the situation into laughter, but you always are there for us to turn a frown up-side-down. When Trey's papaw died, who did he turn to? You! Thank you for blessing our family for so many years, no matter where you are.

I will never forget the football banquet when Coach Mike O'Neill was announced head coach of the Collierville Dragons. Trey was so excited. Mike, you know Trey loved you more than just a coach. He wore the cross necklace you gave him to all his treatments, down to the very end. If players allow it, there can be a special bond between a coach and a player. Trey was blessed by Mike O'Neill. Mike, you have always been so unselfish and have modeled the love of Christ in your own life to the football players. To me, that is a life coach. Our boys are blessed to have you at Collierville. Jay and I are equally blessed to call you and Beth our friends.

Rachel Langston you saved my life! I could not have done this project without you. You took time away from